DAVID'S

STORY:

As Told by Grace Tinker

Nancy Brown

Copyright Page

© 2020 Nancy Brown

First Printing

All rights reserved. Reproduction in whole or part without written permission from the publisher or author is strictly prohibited. Printed in the United States of America.

This book is inspired by the Holy Spirit,
Who teaches us all things.

All Scripture is taken from several versions of the Holy Bible, public domain

Nancy Brown
Moravian Falls, North Carolina

Front cover background photo: © rasica/Adobe Stock

Simply This Publishing
Kindle Direct Publishing

PROLOGUE

  This story is a work of creative non-fiction. That means that this is a true story, but some of the pieces and parts of it that were not completely known, were handled creatively. For example, David's mother is unknown. However we obviously know that David had a mother. We know that she loved him. She named him Ganerdine Erdine Ochir, which means beautiful, strong treasure. She didn't give him up till he was too sick for her to care for. She carried many of the same diseases that he carried and was probably too sick herself to care for him. Because of the diseases that David (and therefore his mother) carried we can readily assume that she picked them up professionally.

  We know that she gave him up because there was no one else to take care of David. There was no husband, no father. There was no family on either side of the family. We know this because Mongolians love their children. They would never give them up. Not even for adoption. Only in the most hopeless case is a child given to another family, but that family must first be adopted into the family that is giving up their child. The two families become one and then the child is placed into the care of its new relatives.

  We know that at the time of David's birth, Mongolia had recently left the Soviet Union to become independent. The Soviets had helped prop up Mongolia's educational system. They had taken children from the countryside and sent them to school in the towns and cities. When the Soviets pulled out of Mongolia, they pulled out their financial support as well. Mongolia struggled to find its feet. With no social welfare system of any type, or money to fund one, children who had lost contact with their families went underground into the steam heat tunnels and either begged for food or prostituted themselves.

From this information we can fill in the blanks about David's mother. That she was sick is a fact. That she gave David up in the most loving way possible is fact. That she had no family to help her is most assuredly fact. What blanks are then left to fill in?

Mongolians are a nomadic people. Even today 2/3rds of the population are country people, living in ghers (or yurts) and tending to their flocks. Her parents were most likely herders. But whether David's mother lost contact with her family or lost her family, we do not know. We do know that in dire circumstances, most people will reconnect with family. That is especially true of Mongolians to whom family is everything. We can know that David's mother's family was lost to her, one way or the other.

We know that only business people and health care workers were allowed into the country at that time. We know that many missionaries went into Mongolia as health care workers and as businessmen. Hence, Anna: her character is purely creative fiction. But once again, we know that there were missionaries, in the form of health care workers, on the ground in

Mongolia. We know that David's mother was seeking health care.

We know that David's mother found Jesus and that she prayed earnestly for her son. How do we know that? We know that because God answered her prayers. Many years and many miles away from the possibility of adopting a child from Mongolia, God gave Grace a clear picture of the child He had waiting for her in Mongolia. Bringing David home wasn't an accident. It wasn't a whim. It was the result of a vision, given to a woman willing and eager to walk in what God had ordained for her and her family. That is the love that God has for us all. He answers our prayers.

While Anna is a created character, David's mother and her parents are not. They certainly existed. Their circumstances in this story are firmly based upon the times and the character of the Mongolian people. Once chapter three is finished, creative non-fiction ends as well. Chapter four begins Grace's story as told by Grace, complete and unalterable, non-fiction. Her vision, her family, her experience with adoption, chemo, and daily life are all hers to tell.

I hope you begin to experience the awesome 'more' of God in your own life as you follow along with Grace on her adventures with Papa. Enjoy the journey.

DAVID'S STORY

"'For I know the plans I have for you,' says the Lord. 'They are for good and not for evil, to give you a future and a hope. In those days, when you pray I will listen. If you look for me in earnest, you will find me when you seek me. I will be found by you,' says the Lord. 'I will end your captivity and restore your fortunes.'" Jeremiah 29:11-14a

TABLE OF CONTENTS

Prologue
Page 3

Chapter I: David's Mother
Page 10

Chapter II: Anna
Page 28

Chapter III: The Storms of Life
Page 39

Chapter IV: The Vision
Page 48

Chapter V: The Vision Continues
Page 55

Chapter VI: A Mothers Love
Page 61

Chapter VII: Who Will Love this Child?
Page 68

Chapter VIII: There is Hope
Page 77

Chapter IX: Decisions
Page 86

Photo Album
Page 96

Chapter X: A Good Strong Name
Page 101

Chapter XI: A Forever Family
Page 106

Chapter XII: Learning to Lean on God
Page 119

Chapter XIII: Chemotherapy
Page 131

Chapter XIV: The Prayer of Others
Page 139

Chapter XV: Mongolia
Page 148

Chapter XVI: The Vision Unfolds
Page 157

Chapter XVII: Growing in Favor with God and Man
Page 168

Chapter XVIII: The Plans I Have for You
Page 176

Chapter XIX: Faith, the Substance of Things Hoped For
Page 186

Chapter XX: Update
Page 190

About The Author
Page 192

Glossary
Page 194

CHAPTER I

David's Mother

A dark, unseen cloud hovered over her head. With malicious intent it clung to her, weaving its tentacles ever more intricately through every fiber of her being. Unrelenting in purpose, evil in intent, darkness staked its claim. When she managed to push through the darkness, the darkness pushed back. It played with her, allowing her an occasional glimpse of sunshine and better days. Most often it held the sunshine at bay. The few faded memories she had managed to retain proved powerless to soothe her anguished soul.

One memory, however, remained sharp. Nothing could cause this precious memory to fade. Each time it arose from the depths of her soul, it loosed her from the darkness, if only for the briefest of moments. This memory alone gave David's mother the strength to go on.

On June 1st, 1999, the sun had shone brightly, as well it should. June 1st is Children's Day in Mongolia, the land of Ghengis Khan. On this day the warm sunshine reflects off the smiles of children and their parents. It dazzles all who witness this Mongolian celebration of its greatest resource – its children. The holiday arrives as this part of the world shakes off the deep freeze of the long cold winter and begins the warming process. All work is suspended. Pretty dresses and brand new clothes are the uniform of the day. Flowers, candy and gifts abound. Children ride the rides at Children's Park. They eat hoshuur and buuz, national dishes, till they can stand no more. It's a day to share love with family. It's a day to make memories.

On just this day in 1999, David arrived. He took his first shallow breath. A startled gasp escaped his lips as hot dusty air dug into his newly formed lungs. His first taste of life gave little promise.

Simultaneously, a long, deep moan resonated throughout the gher, the traditional Mongolian home. The sound drowned out David's pitiful gasp. Drenched to the bone with sweat, David's mother lay motionless. Only the sound she made gave evidence that there was life yet within her.

Slowly she roused herself. She reached for her child and held him close. Quiet sobbing gave way to tears of delight. The sound of unrestrained joy emanated slowly from her throat till it reached a crescendo that pierced the very air that now filled David's lungs. Love flowed from mother to son. A male child had been born to David's mother. All would be well.

A boy born on Children's Day is an auspicious sign. No sunnier day ever existed in David's mother's young memory. The unseen cloud waited, not far off, but David's mother only saw the sunshine. She only remembered the sunshine. She remembered the joy. She remembered her beautiful baby boy. The smile on her thin, young face revealed all there was to tell. This day gave her hope for a future which she had until now only dreamt of.

Memories are meant to be made on Children's Day. David's mother now enjoyed the best of all possible memories feasibly acquired on this particular day. She counted this blessing a propitious sign. She had been highly favored. Good fortune no longer eluded her. Her confidence soared. Maybe now the darkness would be compelled to retreat.

A new life.

A new hope.

It was indeed a propitious sign.

....

Generally speaking, David's mother bore a disconsolate air. More child than woman in years or sophistication, yet she resembled more a woman than a child in trial and experience. Misfortune had followed her most of her life.

Born to a poor herder family from the far end of the aimag, she had spent her early childhood engulfed in the tender warmth of her family's love. Like most Mongolians, she deeply relished the adulation of family. Her time with them, though of short duration and now long past, remained among the dearest of her memories, but that was all they were. They were memories from a distant past she could never recover. They were memories on which the dark cloud had imperceptibly advanced.

Like all Mongolian children of that era, David's mother had gone east at a tender age to attend school in the city. It had been hard to leave her family, the fire warming the gher, the great starry sky, the open grasslands, and her father playing his beloved morin khuur. Her mother had tucked her into bed each night with a gentle kiss that warmed her throughout those long Mongolian nights. David's mother clung to these memories. Who wouldn't? Though fading, they still retained the power to warm her thoughts if not her extremities. She longed to share this warm glow of tender affection with the newborn child cradled in her arms. For David's mother, the glowing embers of once bright memories were all she had left to share with her son.

When she was young, a snowstorm had claimed her father's life. The storm had arrived early in the season. It came without warning. Her father had ventured into the storm to bring in the sheep. Herders realize early on that the welfare of their family depends upon the well-being of their herd.

He never returned.

They discovered his body several days later, frozen to the ground where he had dropped from exhaustion. The blinding fury of the storm had disoriented this self-sufficient herder, a man who had prided himself on the skills he had acquired early in life, the skills essential for survival in this forbidding land.

The storm had disappeared as quickly as it had arrived. Nothing had changed really. The sun still rose. The sheep still grazed. David's mother was still a young girl, alone in the big city. She still attended school like thousands of other lonely young children.

No, nothing had changed, except now a lonely young girl no longer had a father.

Sitting on her hard bed in the cold concrete dorm room, the news of her father's death hit David's mother as hard as the storm had hit her father. It hit her with a blinding fury. It then left her there, empty and hollow, feeling the same numbness one feels from prolonged exposure to the deep Mongolian cold. Like her father, she never felt warm again. But, unlike her father she kept on living.

Like her father before her, she kept on doing what she needed to do. She did what was required of her. Like her father who had gone out to tend the sheep, she continued to get up every day and go on with her education. Her father could have abandoned the sheep, let them take care of themselves. He could have hoped for the best. He didn't do that. He was responsible for those sheep. David's mother could have curled up in a ball and refused to go to classes. She could have gone to classes and stared listlessly at the board. For a while she did just that. Then reality set in. Taking care of her mother was now her responsibility. She couldn't just hope for the best. She had to do her best. Like her father, she did what she had to do. She hoped he would be proud.

This burden consumed her. She counted the days till late spring when she could go home for the summer and help her mother with the sheep. The aroma of her mother's cooking wafted through her memory, helping console her. The thought of curling up in her mother's warm embrace did as well. They would laugh together. They would cry together. They would share good memories. David's mother would at last feel warm again. She waited desperately for that day to come.

It never did.

Soon after the death of her father, David's mother received the news that her beloved mother had also passed away. The letter from a neighbor possessed few details. Perhaps she had passed away from food poisoning, perhaps from grief or depression or despair. Either way, she was gone.

Sitting alone on her small, hard bed in the cold, concrete dorm, for a second time, David's mother quivered. This second storm had forsaken her of all human touch. A deep loneliness now encompassed the core of her being. The unfathomable had happened and it had happened to her. She longed to be comforted by the sound of her father's singing or the warm, soft touch of her mother's gentle hand. Darkness hovered over her. David's young mother succumbed to the realization that these things would never happen for her again. A soft groan escaped her lips. Sensing opportunity, darkness took its foothold in her soul. It told her that she, herself, was all that she had left. She was now her own responsibility. David's mother quivered again, but tears never came. Tears are an unaffordable luxury in the darkness.

In spite of all that had occurred, David's mother understood that her life still held promise. Of this, her teachers and dorm supervisor ever reminded her. She still possessed the opportunity to acquire a good education. She excelled at academics. She could expect reasonable employment. A husband of her choosing and her own beautiful, happy family were yet possible. These were the hopes, the dreams, the possibilities that David's mother clung to as she struggled through school without parents to go home to in the late spring, without parents to send her warm clothes during the long, brutal winter.

"My time will come," she consoled herself. "I just need to wait. I need to do what needs to be done. I need to get a good education. I need to secure my future."

She clung to her hopes for the future as fiercely as she embraced her memories of the past. Hopes and memories, each of them helped sustain her throughout the long, lonely days and the even longer nights. Such is the optimism of youth. A young orphaned girl abides, awaiting all that should rightly be hers, expecting a home, a family and love. How many other young children, orphaned or discarded in Asia or anywhere else on this globe for that matter, share this same optimism, this same hope? Is it not the same hope we all carry? Home, family, love......

For David's mother that day never arrived. The Soviets withdrew from Mongolia soon after the Berlin Wall fell. Despite its serious lack of experience in self-government, Mongolia, a former Soviet Satellite State, became a democracy overnight. Corruption, handed down from a Communist system, left the country rife with politicians fighting each other for personal gain. With little of its own capital and even less knowledge of how to turn natural resources into finances, funds for such things as orphan education grew scarce. Lacking funds, many boarding schools were forced to close. The state could no longer afford to keep them all running.

Children were sent home to their families. Their education either ended or resumed at a later date. Many older children, long estranged from their parents and grown used to the comforts of city living, stayed on in the city. They found jobs, or begged, or begged jobs to keep themselves alive. Many, like David's mother, slipped through the cracks. They were lost and forgotten. They were young children – left alone in the streets to take care of themselves.

Of such were the street children of Ulaan Baatar made. They were young, orphaned, abandoned children, children who dreamed of homes and families, children whose dreams faded into poverty, sickness, disease, and approaching adulthood. They begged during the day and huddled underground in the steam pipe tunnels at night for warmth. They formed a community of children, the steam tunnel children. Even today, in this country of 2.5 million, 4,000 children are said to be abandoned.

....

The steam plant was several miles outside of town. Miles and miles of underground tunnels had been dug under the city through which the steam pipes meandered, servicing every building in town. The tunnels were large enough to stand up in, to move around in, and to put down old cardboard to sleep on.

They were readily accessed through the man-hole covers on the sidewalks in town. Most important of all, the tunnels were warm.

With no other options available, David's mother entered this community.

Begging may sustain the body, but rarely does it sustain the soul. It tears away at hope for something better. It shreds the best of intentions. It mutilates dignity and self-esteem. When a clean cardboard box to sleep in becomes coveted, becomes worth fighting for, becomes your hope for tomorrow, then larger dreams perish. They cease to exist.

With little else for an uneducated girl to do except beg, David's mother again, did what she had to do to survive. She begged. There was, of course, something else she could do. Prostitution paid better than begging and opportunities of this sort abound for attractive young women. Yet, despite all that had befallen her, David's young mother continued to embrace hopes of meeting a handsome young man who would love her and pursue her with all of his heart. She imagined having children and a home.

"One day," she often told herself, "one day, things will change. I don't need to sell my body."

"Nothing will change. You will sell your body." The darkness stroked her long black hair as it whispered back.

For many years begging sustained David's mother. As street children get older, begging brings in less and less money. *"Get a job,"* is proffered in place of food or money. Some manage to do just that. The rest steal food and money from the younger children. Worse yet, they use the younger children to beg for them, and then discard them when they are too old to beg. As begging leaves no time for education, these children then need to find or beget other children to bring in money. The cycle perpetuates itself.

It's a game of survival.

No one wins.

All too soon David's mother ripened into womanhood. She had become too old to beg. Small jobs helped sustain her, however little. More often, hunger flashed its ugly fangs, revealing the darkness and its impatient desire for control. The cold, hard dormitory bed she had once detested now seemed a luxury beyond her grasp. The warmth of her mother's touch was now only a dim and fading memory.

David's mother had resisted the ways of the streets longer than most young girls in her position. She had seen other girls slink into dark places with strange men. *"This is a way out of life in the tunnels,"* everyone said. *"Men will pay to spend time with you. You might have to do things you didn't want to do, but you can make enough money to live in an apartment. Maybe you could get your own gher. Everyone does it. You may as well get paid."*

Beautiful young women lacking money or education often sell themselves cheaply. No matter how beautiful you are, you need clean hair and clean clothes and perhaps some perfume, for someone to pay more than a pittance to spend time with you. To make enough to sustain yourself, perhaps even to prosper, you need some knowledge of what you are worth.

David's mother possessed none of these things. She had no money to spare on the public bathhouse. She wasn't certain what perfume was. All self-worth had faded with her memories. What price could she place on someone whom even God seemed to have forgotten?

Hunger and darkness had their way with her. *"You're worth a scrap of bread."*

"What does it matter? You're going to be dead soon anyhow."

"You'd better take what you can get."

"Maybe if you get better at it people will pay more."

Like all too many before her, she sold herself for whatever she could get.

Scraping together enough money to live in a small gher outside of town took only a short time. David's mother shared the gher with several other women. Her self-affirming mantra, *"It's better than the tunnels,"* helped her convince herself that all was well.

"It's still working the streets," darkness pointed out. *"No one loves you. No one even cares. You're just a cheap prostitute."*

Still, it paid the bills. Hunger, no longer crouching at their door, was long forgotten. Although they had no running water, they did have electricity. They could buy a television if they chose. They had beds, real beds – even if they were used far more for work than for rest. Compared to the tunnels, this life above ground invigorated David's mother. Roses returned to her cheeks. Light danced in her eyes. Darkness was forced to retreat. Hope, ever ready to rebound, reflected itself in her every move.

Everything wasn't perfect, of course. Sometimes David's mother had to stand outside for an eternity when a roommate brought a customer to the gher. That was the least of it. Unnecessary roughness was not unexpected in this type of business. Thievery was rife. The type of men that engaged this type of service exuded unsavory behavior. Drunks; Thieves; Perverts; and unfaithful husbands looking for services in a way that a wife won't provide: A man who will buy a woman doesn't need to respect her. He just wants his money's worth. Then he might want his money back. The neighbors knew what they were doing and offered neither help nor sympathy. They were scorned women. They knew why. They knew what they were.

....

Occasionally the police picked them up for prostitution. More often the police were customers – the kind of customers who don't pay. The girls were forced to pay them and to pay them often. *"For protection,"* the police snickered, but it was no joking matter. So the girls paid. They paid corruption with corruption. They rendered their bodies. They seared their hearts. They relinquished their souls. In the end it didn't really matter. In this business, you pay a price for every customer entertained. Tiny slivers ripped from the soul are left to wither and die with each tugrik earned. So slowly and imperceptibly does this process transpire that it is hard to perceive. One day you awaken as from a long deep sleep. You shake off the cobwebs. With a sudden clarity you become aware that not an ounce of your soul remains.

This realization had freshly dawned on David's mother the day she met Anna.

David's mother was ill. She hadn't felt well for a long time. Sure, the move from the tunnels to a life above ground had been invigorating. It had been glorious, if only for a short while. Minus that small exception, if memory served, there wasn't a time when David's mother remembered feeling well. Not since that first fierce snowstorm had taken her father, had the darkness relented. Prostitution had torn away her soul. Loneliness had choked her heart. Yet this was something worse. Disease now wracked her malnourished body.

She'd heard of a free clinic where they took care of women like her. They didn't ask any questions. It was operated by strangers who were foreigners; Christians.

Different forms of Christianity had been scattered throughout Mongolia since the time of Ghengis Khan. A Christian church had operated in Kharhorum, the heart of Ghengis's empire, the capitol of the largest empire to ever exist.

Since Communist times, most Mongolian people considered themselves either Buddhist or atheist. Those who considered themselves Buddhist didn't practice Buddhism. They observed a few Buddhist traditions, but knew little of Buddha's teachings. Like Christian teaching, Buddhist teaching had long been stamped out. The Communists had seen to that. No one believed much in God here in Mongolia. Since Communism fell, foreigners had begun to trickle in. Some came for the mines, seeking copper and gold and diamonds. Some came for adventure, and these were often the customers that paid the best. Some came to talk about their god to people like David's mother, who needed help and couldn't afford it. If you could stand to listen politely, you could get help.

David's mother needed help.

She had attempted seeking help at the State Hospital several times. They knew her there. They knew what she did for a living. Though some were sympathetic, most expressed the opinion that she was a waste of good time and scarce resources. They told her that she would die and probably sooner than later. Facts manifest eager prophets. Prostitutes face an early demise. Her reputation prevailed. Fate loomed, inescapable. Maybe she could get help at the foreign clinic.

So, this is how David's mother met Anna - sick, scared and soulless. If ever David's mother needed help, it was now. If ever there was someone who wanted to help, it was Anna.

Freshly scrubbed and painted, the foreign clinic emanated light and cleanliness. It radiated warmth and friendliness. In this place there existed far too much light and warmth for a woman of the streets to feel comfortable. David's mother shuddered. Looking around, she spotted a woman with whom she was familiar. They made no eye contact. Inhaling deeply and holding her breath, David's mother took a seat.

The receptionist took what little information David's mother offered. No phone number. No true address.

No occupation. No known relatives. What more was there to say?

They took a blood sample and a urine sample and told David's mother to come back in a week. This week dragged slowly for David's mother. Self-examination gave way to self-pity.

"Why bother to go back? I'm just going to die either way."

"Why not bother? What else am I going to do?"

"I'm not worth it."

"No one cares."

"Who would miss me?"

"Why did my life turn out this way?"
"For what reason am I still alive?"

"Just give up and die."

Relentless thoughts pursued David's mother. Darkness dug deep. Depression reigned. Even so, she chose to return to the clinic. She didn't know why she went back, but she did. She had no place else to go. She was too sick to do anything else. She may as well sit in a bright, clean office for a while. It was nice there. She felt better there than she had in a long time. She liked that. So, she went back.

....

David's mother checked in. She sighed as she waited. She knew she was sick. She knew the life she had chosen would be the end of her. Nothing changes. The prophets were right. Girls like her die young. They pay for their clothes and TV's and their ghers not only with their bodies and souls, but also with their lives. Maybe this was the way out of a life she had never really lived, an early end to a life so miserably spent, waiting, hoping, and dreaming of something better.

Maybe she didn't care. Maybe she was tired. Maybe she was ready to see an end to all she had suffered. But then why did she seek help? Maybe the optimism she had clung to for so long had crept back into her life. Only recently one of her roommates had found a man to love her. He rescued her from the streets. He took her as his wife. Life was hard, but this man worked harder. They built a home. They were building a family. Maybe......

Anna walked in, interrupting this daydream. Bright and cheery as this freshly scrubbed room, self-confidence radiated from her smile. It made her glow. An inner strength, drawn from deep within her soul dominated the room. This was the kindest, gentlest face David's mother had seen since her own mother passed away.

"Here is a woman who has not sold her soul." David's mother's leaned forward as this thought danced across her mind. She was unwillingly drawn to this smiling woman. *"This is the type of woman I wish I could be."*

How long had she needed the presence of an older woman to guide her, to direct her, to comfort her, to talk to her, to encourage her? Could this be happening? Who was this kind woman? Was it too much to hope that this woman, smiling so gently at her, could help her?

For the first time in a long time David's mother relaxed. In front of her stood a woman who didn't know her, a woman who didn't condemn her, and a woman whose smile made her feel at home. At home – a place she hadn't been in too many years. David's mother sat back and relaxed. She bathed herself in the warm glow of home, in the encompassing river of love flowing from the smile of a foreigner.

Anna looked briefly at David's mother. Though her smile never changed, she was shocked at what she saw. The chart indicated that this girl was seventeen. This gaunt, hollow-cheeked girl might have looked thirty on her best day. Perhaps there was a mistake.

Anna sighed. She knew there was no mistake. It didn't matter anyhow. The outcome was the same regardless of age. David's mother tested positive for Hepatitis B. She tested positive for Hepatitis C. She tested positive for Syphilis. Malnourishment was the least of her problems.

Anna knew well how these diseases were contracted. David's mother had sold herself again and again just to survive. This road disguised as survival stands as it has always stood, destined to doom unto death any weary traveler who falls prey its easy deception.

Anna had seen so many young girls come through the clinic. All suffered health problems stemming from this lifestyle. Yet, David's still beautiful, young mother stood out from among them all. Her age alone should have spared her from an intimate acquaintance with untimely demise. Deception and death are, however, willing partners to all who choose them. So, here before Anna, sat David's newly hopeful mother - impoverished, diseased, malnourished, exhausted, and pregnant.

Anna looked into those deep brown eyes so full of hope. Her heart broke within her. Anna was a Christian. She knew her God. She understood that

God could bring healing to David's mother. She also grasped how sick David's mother was.

Silently she spoke to her God. *"Please dear Father, show yourself to this girl. Make yourself real to her. Make yourself known to her. Show her your love.*

Show her your promises. Bring her healing. Bring her hope. And please, Lord, please, watch over this innocent child she is carrying."

CHAPTER II

Anna

The bond between David's mother and Anna had been instant. A young girl searching for love not found in a physical relationship and an older woman with children grown and love to spare can share a powerful bond. In this case, as in others, two people from entirely different backgrounds, entirely different worlds, simply met each other's needs.

This bond of love blossomed further as these two women walked together through the last few months of David's mother's life. Anna, so well educated and respected, spent herself caring for those who were unable to care for themselves. David's mother, so poor in spirit, so damaged in soul and body, soaked up every affection offered. Love grew with every grace exchanged.

Love encourages. Love builds. Love multiplies. Not surprisingly, a sense of self-worth began to grow in David's mother.

Anna secured a place for David's mother at a nearby woman's shelter. She gave her a job cleaning the office on the days she felt well enough to work. She welcomed David's mother into her home for dinner or tea in the evenings. Together they spent hours talking and sharing the things of their hearts.

Anna spoke to David's mother about the love of God. She unfolded God's plan of creation, the world first, then man, in God's own image. She expounded on His deep, abiding love for that which He alone created. *"It's about us,"* Anna whispered. *"It's always been about us. God loves us. We are His creation. We are His people. We are His alone."*

She explained the almighty awesomeness of God. *"God is good and perfect and holy and righteous and we are not worthy to even come close to such righteousness and purity. He loves us, but we are filthy with sin. All of us. Not one of us has right to come before such a righteous God. We need to be clean and holy and right with God. We need forgiveness from all our filth, the sin we have chosen over a relationship with God. God sees our sin, our mess, our unworthiness, but He still wants a relationship with us. So He made a plan. He sent His Son, Jesus, to be a sacrifice for our sins. Not unlike the blood of animals sacrificed on altars of old for forgiveness of sin, the blood of the Son is our covering, our covenant with God. This covenant, this blood of Jesus, our Redeemer, paid the price for all of it. It's a done deal. We are sinners no more. We are worthy. We are righteous. We are loved. We are His."*

David's mother knew that she had too much sin in her life to be worthy of the God who had created her. She had sold her body. She had sold her soul. Grateful as she was for Anna's loving kindness, the secure knowledge that God Eternal loved her remained elusive.

The darkness floating round David's mother roused itself. A vigorous battle ensued. Doubts and questions, like arrows shot through her mind. *"If God loves me then why has my life been wasted? Why am I going to die now that I've found Anna? Why have I been born to live this life? How could this be love?"*

Anna watched David's mother struggle with her thoughts. She had struggled similarly herself years before. *"It's Ok,"* Anna soothed her. *"It takes a while to sink in sometimes. We all struggle from time to time. We are allowed to question God. God doesn't always keep bad things from happening. There can be consequences to our choices, but He is always there to help us. We just need to let Him in."*

"But how do you have a relationship with God?" David's mother shook her head. She wanted what Anna had. She wanted it for herself and she wanted it for her unborn child.

"God requires a blood sacrifice for sin. All religions have copied this. All religions require sacrifice. It's not a new idea. It's just that God did it for us. And if God does it – well, it's pretty much done."

David's mother understood sacrifices. She had seen Buddhists burn money for their ancestors and leave food for them. They built piles of rocks and walked around them, praying. She wasn't sure why they did it. She had tried it herself a few times, but the effort had proven useless. She chuckled at herself.

"I've seen that too," Anna chuckled along with David's mother, her head bobbing up and down in

agreement. She'd seen the piles of rocks and the turquoise sashes. *"Buddha was a very great man. He said so many good things. Most importantly, he said that he was not God. He never claimed to be God. How can a man who is not God answer people's prayers?"*

"I guess he can't." David's mother turned this information over in her mind. *"Tell me more."*

"Since God required the sacrifice, God provided the sacrifice. He is a just God. He sent His son Jesus to earth to live a sinless, blameless life. That's why He is called the 'Lamb of God.' He was the perfect sacrifice – just like a lamb needs to be perfect to be a sacrifice. He was the final sacrifice. We no longer need to sacrifice animals. We just need Jesus."

"But how can Jesus be our sacrifice? We didn't make any sacrifice."

"He did it for us. All we have to do is receive it."

David's mother was bewildered. *"How do you do that?"*

Anna smiled at David's mother. *"If your country wins a war, do you say 'the soldiers won' or do you say 'we won'? If a Mongolian wins a gold medal at the Olympics do you say 'he won' or 'we won'? You say it either way. You can give victory to the victor or you can claim it for yourself."*

We can say, "'Jesus died' or we can say 'Jesus died for me'. We can claim that victory."

"When someone dies and leaves you an inheritance, do you watch someone else claim it or do you claim what was meant for you?"

"Well.....I would claim it, of course." This concept was new to David's mother. Her inheritance, the family home, all the animals, had disappeared. She hadn't been there to claim them. Maybe this did make sense. Maybe you do need to claim what is given you. Hope again rose from the depths of her still young soul.

Panicking as he felt his grip loosening, Darkness summoned Depression and Despair. Together they raised the question of worth. David's mother had nothing. She had given nothing. She had nothing to give. She was worthless. How could she claim this gift, this inheritance, this sacrifice for her sins? What did it mean if she did?

Experienced in the tactics of the enemy of Truth, Anna chose love and patience. She repeated again the plan of God in all its simplicity. *"We are all sinners. No one is worthy of God's forgiveness without sacrifice. That is why Jesus came to earth – to be that sacrifice – to be our Savior. If we claim Jesus as our Savior, we are forgiven of all our sins."*

"If you believe in your heart that Jesus is Lord and Savior, then you are saved. It's as easy as that. Just receive this forgiveness. Make it your own. Say, 'I believe there is a God. I believe He loves me. I believe He sent His son Jesus to die for me. Jesus is my sacrifice. I am forgiven.' This forgiveness is for everyone. We can all have a relationship with God."

These words shed anew the light in David's mother's heart, but darkness cannot abide in light. It dug deeper. Confusion was summoned. As it entwined itself around her thoughts, a relationship with God, the desire of her heart, again escaped her comprehension.

"I believe there is a god. The world didn't just happen. People didn't just suddenly form." David's mother sorted her thoughts out loud. *"And I believe that if He created us, He must love us. That makes sense to me."* She rubbed her growing stomach. She loved the child she carried inside of her, the child she had created, this child she had never met. How much more could God love those He had created?

"And I believe that any being that could create the universe must be all knowing and all powerful – He must be God."

"And I believe that he made us for a purpose – or He wouldn't have made us. He's too smart for that. And I believe that He wants to be part of our lives. I can see that He's a part of your life, Anna. I can see love and peace and joy. If that's having God in your life, then I want it. But can just claiming Jesus as my Lord and Savior make me whole again? I've given myself away piece by piece. Can God do that? Can He make me whole?" Woe pushed confusion aside. Tears gathered in David's mother's eyes. *"Does He really want to have a relationship with me?"*

"Of course He does!" Anna reached out to encourage David's mother. *"He loves us all. But we all get to choose. He won't force anything on us. We each get to

choose. Jesus did the work. He paid the price. He went to the cross. He won the victory. Because of His blood, His covering, His forgiveness, we get to spend eternity with Him in heaven after our earthly death. This is a promise. All we need to do is ask Him to be a part of our lives and then let Him in."

"Believe and receive? It seems too simple."

"It is that simple. And that's not the best part."

"There's more?"

"Yes, of course." Anna's eyes twinkled. Her joy was now infectious. *"When you ask Jesus into your life the promises are unending. Peace. Love. Joy. Family. Relationships. You get eternity in heaven with Him and a relationship with Him now."*

"What's it like? Do you talk to God? Does He answer you? Is that why you are happy?"

"Well, yeah, I do talk to God. And, yes, He does answer me. It's called prayer. I talk to God all the time. He answers me in so many different ways."

"How?"

The Bible tells us that faith comes by hearing God's words, and David's mother was hearing God's words. Anna saw to that. As faith grew, darkness began to shrink away. Depression dissipated. Despair disappeared. Woe succumbed to joy. Confusion held on, but not without struggle.

"How does He answer you?"

"Sometimes I hear Him quietly pointing things out. Sometime I see the works of His hands, the things He has done for me. Sometimes I just feel impressed to pray for people and I see my prayers answered. Sometimes, when I read my Bible, God talks to me through His written Word. Sometimes He just brings people into my life; people like you my dear sweet child. I see God in you."

"How can you see God in me? I am not a Christian."

"Yes you are. You believe that Jesus died for us. Jesus has forgiven you – you just haven't accepted His forgiveness yet."

Confusion struggled to retain its hold.

"Whether or not you forgive yourself – He's forgiven you. Whether or not you accept His forgiveness – He's forgiven you. Accept His forgiveness and start walking in it. The Bible tells us that your soul is worth more to God than the whole world. If you were the only person on earth, Jesus would still have died for you."

"How come no one has ever told me this before?"

"Ohhh," Anna sighed softly. She shook her head. *"He's always been with you. He gave you parents that loved you so that you would know what love was like. He's given you a child to love that will love you back. He held you in His arms every time you cried yourself to sleep. He's always been there. You*

just didn't know it. And now He's sent me to tell you about Him. You have been on His heart and His mind all of your life."

Truth sheds light on every situation. Confusion could no longer block the light. David's mother knew in her heart that what she was hearing was true. Looking back she realized that she had felt the presence of God many times in her life. When she was cold and someone had given her something warm to wear - this was the hand of God. When she was hungry and someone had given her food to eat - this was God watching over her. Was it God who had comforted her when she was sad and lonely? Looking back she knew she had never been alone. Jesus had always been there with her. She lowered her head and asked Jesus to come into her life.

Like many who accept Jesus as Lord and Savior David's mother wondered why she had never seen His hand on her life before. She wondered how many other people miss seeing Jesus in their lives.

....

The warm, inviting atmosphere of Anna's home brought a healing balm to the soul. Long talks with Anna lifted the heart. David's mother grew stronger and stronger in this curative atmosphere. She no longer needed to walk the streets at all hours of the night. She no longer needed to carry water or coal for miles to the gher. She could rest when she was weary. Rest and good nutrition were a sound prescription for restoration. As youth and vitality regained vigor, self-confidence and self-respect blossomed as well. The road to recovery became the new path chosen.

The child inside of David's mother grew and grew. Unsearchable joy, uncontained gratitude filled her heart to its fullest whenever thoughts of this child caressed her mind. At last, a child to call her own. This child meant everything. She would love this child forever. She would give it all the love that had been lost to her.

David's mother could have chosen abortion. Many young girls in her situation did. Termination provides a convenient end to many an inconvenient pregnancy. Her options for self-sufficiency hadn't improved. Some in her situation, choosing not to abort, used their babies to beg. Others left their babies or small children alone for hours in the cold gher while they went to work. She didn't understand how, but faith had started working within her. She knew God had a plan. She knew it was a good plan.

It might be hard, but doubts no longer assailed David's mother. She would keep her baby. She would love it. She was Mongolian and Mongolians love their children. No exceptions would be found here. New life contained within itself new hope for the future.

As faith grows, hope abounds.

Maybe now, maybe now that she believed that Jesus was Lord and Savior, things would change. They had already changed hadn't they? David's mother now had Anna. A new baby would love her. She had Jesus in her life. She was growing stronger every day. Anna said that school was a possibility when she felt well enough. Maybe now, maybe now it wasn't just a hope, a dream. Maybe things had changed

CHAPTER III

The Storms of Life

The storms of life fret not over the unprepared. They scorn inadequacy. They rage undaunted. They taunt. They defy us to go on.

God will allow such storms in our lives from time to time, to test us, to teach us. Will we allow the storm to rule over us? Will we lean on our own strength and understanding? Will we embrace Jesus and entrust to Him our problems?

"Look to Jesus, honey. Always look to Jesus. A word from Him will calm any storm." Anna gently mentored her eager new student, training her in God's truth.

Praying can be a new concept, an uncomfortable shift in thought or behavior, for those not schooled in the process. *"Talking to yourself,"* Doubt insisted. *"Words tossed to the wind... And listening for an answer? Who does that? You'll look like a fool."*

Eagerness gave itself to pride and pride to self-pity and self-pity to belligerence, a common trinity which feeds itself upon itself, a constantly spinning circle within which there is no easy escape. Taking control, belligerence inserted itself into the conversation. *"I just don't know how to pray!!!"*

"Score one for us!" Belligerence and Pride high fived.

Self-pity sighed.

This blow, aimed for Anna, missed its mark. Wisdom rose, flowing through her like a stream in the desert, unexpected and refreshing. It took no prisoners. *"You know how to beg don't you? If you can ask strangers for food or shelter, how much more can you ask from your Heavenly Father who loves you?"*

Embarrassed, David's mother recoiled. She didn't enjoy thinking about the past. She didn't want to hear about it, from Anna or anyone.

"The Bible tells us that we have not, because we ask not. If you've got a problem – go right to Jesus and tell Him about it. Ask for help. He always answers our prayers. Maybe not always the way we want him to, but He always answers our prayers."

"OK! OK! OK!" David's mother shut down. She turned away. She would never discuss that subject with Anna again.

And she didn't. She never had the chance. Anna fell a few days later.

An undisguised mine field, the sidewalks of Ulaan Baator in that day lay in wait for unwitting victims. Children were taught from an early age to mind where they were walking. Adults kept a vigilant eye over every step taken. The sidewalk pavers rolled like the waves of the ocean, sometimes in gentle fashion, sometimes breaking into chaos as onto the shore. Many pavers, removed for repairs, were never replaced. Loose gravel filled the gaps. Manhole covers, taken for their value in scrap iron or left open for easier access into the tunnels, left yawning holes, ready to devour the inattentive meanderer. A carefree stroll down the street in Ulaan Baatar portended misfortune. It was simply ill advised.

Anna, ever prayerful, lifted her eyes as she walked. An intense conversation with her Lord engulfed her thoughts. The warmth of His presence flooded her being. She floated down the street, forgetting the ever present danger of rippling sidewalks and open manholes. Without warning or fanfare the avoidable occurred. Anna missed her step and fell.

Rushed to the hospital with a shattered hip and a few cracked ribs, little could be done. With uncertain internal injuries suspected, the best option, all agreed, was Korea. Before amends could be made or goodbyes could be said, Anna was whisked away. Another storm had raged over David's mother's life. A fresh wound now rent her heart.

David's mother's newfound faith wavered. Doubt again assailed her. *"How can this happen to such a godly woman? Where was God in all of this? Is God really real?"*

Anna's gentle voice whispered in David's mother's ear. *"Our God is good. He is Love. He is Faithful and Just. There is no evil in Him. No bad thing can ever come from Him."*

David's mother leaned in to listen more closely. *"We do have an enemy though, whose purpose it is to rob, kill and destroy. He delights in hurting us because we are the beloved of the Father."*

Anna's soft voice continued, *"When we are hurting, our Father who loves us, hurts with us and holds us even closer. He collects our tears. It is not His will or desire for any bad thing to happen to us. But if, or when, these things do happen, we know that it is our Father's will to turn them around for us. His Word promises us that all things work together for good for those who love the Lord; for those who are called according to His purposes. We who love Him are 'the called ones'."*

Memories of all that Anna had taught her came flooding back to David's mother. *"We just need to trust Him. He has a plan."* Peace gently descended onto David's mother, covering her like a soft, warm blanket.

Half asleep on the job, Darkness now awoke to this new situation. This wasn't the plan. This could not be allowed. Snapping to attention, he seized upon unforeseen opportunity and crept back with uncanny stealth. Doubt redoubled his offensive as well, attacking truth, thickening himself around David's mother, peeling back the blanket of Peace. In grief, in darkness, in doubt, David's mother chose not to embrace Jesus. Neither did she allow the storm to reign over her. She'd weathered more than a few storms by now. This was no different. She knew whose strength to lean on. Her own. She would do what she had to do.

....

Without an advocate, there was no way to continue to support herself where she was. David's mother chose to move back to the gher outside of town. She was welcomed by old familiar faces and new ones, fresh from the tunnels. Life there had remained, for the most part, unchanged.

Her time being imminent, the girls asked little of David's mother. The burden she supposed herself to be, however, weighed heavily on her mind. Determined not to be an imposition, she asked even less of them.

"I can do this. I can do this. I can do this." David's mother entertained no other thoughts.

And she did.

David made his appearance a few hours after the sun rose that first day in June, 1999. It was Children's Day. It had been barely a month since Anna had departed for Korea. No fanfare blasted. No celebration resounded through the dusty air. The sound of silence filled the neighborhood. Mothers and Fathers were off with their children to Children's Park to enjoy the holiday. Working girls were working. One quiet young woman from the gher had chosen to remain with David's mother. This proved providential.

David's mother was again malnourished. Not wanting to be a burden, she had eaten little. Lacking proper nutrition, her health had deteriorated. Her baby was the only thing that kept her moving forward. Her baby kept her from relinquishing herself to poverty, disease, self-loathing and death. She had a reason to live. She was having a baby.

Unattended, this difficult process could have taken an ugly turn, but David's mother was familiar with pain. She knew how to weather a storm. She held on. Jesus knelt beside her, unseen, guiding the young woman who had remained behind. Though He waited for David's mother to call on Him, she never discerned His presence. An emotional fortress, built to withhold love, human or divine, surrounded her. She continued to rely on herself alone.

Disproportionate to his spindly body, David's sizeable head had given his small framed mother a rough time. Jolt upon jolt of pain unimaginable wracked her frail body. Darkness cackled and danced. Her final hours could prove to be his finest. Consciousness floated away. Watching her lie on the bed with her unborn child, darkness envisioned a double prize. He strengthened his unholy grasp. Eternal darkness threatened both mother and son.

All Heaven watched. All heaven waited. Creatures great and small held their collective breath. A bitter battle ensued. Darkness congealed like tar around mother and son, impenetrable, unforgiving, and victorious at last. Light could not shatter this darkness. No shreds of truth could penetrate this covering. Tar does not disperse.

When all seemed lost, Jesus himself donned the breastplate of righteousness. The sword of truth, gleaming in His right hand, pierced through the heavy shroud threatening to smother both mother and son. He laid open the tarry substance and light entered in. Of necessity, darkness ceded its grip. Life on earth was sustained for the time being. Long before earth or time began, it seems, Jesus had laid other plans for

David and his mother. Decreed by God, time yet remained for both of them.

....

Afterwards, David's mother lay exhausted on the bed for weeks. Grateful for sustenance and nurture, she repeatedly thanked those around her. She heaped praise on the girl who had assisted the birthing process. However, she never acknowledged the One who carried her through this difficult birth. She never thanked the One who gave His life so that she could live, the One who gave her a chance to hold her cherished son.

It never occurred to her.

While she did not embrace Jesus, David's mother's thoughts were no longer on herself alone. They were on this child that she had so long awaited. They were on this baby that could change her life. It was a boy! A boy could grow up big and strong. A boy could help with the chores. A boy, she could love forever. She foresaw her future in this tiny child. It was as rosy a future as ever a young mother dared imagined. She sighed and held him close.

David was born with big Mongolian baby cheeks and soft brown hair that stuck up on his head. Nature had endowed him with big brown eyes and smooth olive skin. Like his mother, he was pleasant to behold. Possessed by a sweet and gentle nature this child carried an air of divine affinity. He was special. He was a child of God.

David's mother called him Ganerdene Erdene Ochir. It meant beautiful, strong treasure. A good name portends the future. He was beautiful, but he needed to be strong as well; strong for both of them. And above all else, she treasured him.

Much anticipated, born in love, David had finally arrived.

Happiness exists as a state of mind. David's mother couldn't rise from her bed. Feverish, unable to eat, disease as well as childbirth had taken its toll. Yet happiness abounded from deep within her. Joy filled her replenished soul. She had waited years and years for this. She had wanted a husband and her own home first, but she had a son, a strong, handsome son. She was happy.

David's birth renewed his mother's hope for the future. His mother counted this day as a blessing. It was a good sign to have a son born on Children's Day in Mongolia. Maybe now.....

For the first time in her life she prayed. She did so without realizing it. She more thought it than said it aloud, but the words were audible. *"Thank you, God, for this son. And God, if you are real, please take care of my baby."*

God heard her and answered her prayer. He'd been waiting for it.

God always answers prayer. Often enough we don't see the answers to our prayers, but they are still answered. There is no mystery to this. There is just a

God who loves us and is waiting to help us if we will call on Him.

David's mother had just called on Him.

CHAPTER IV

The Vision

Eight thousand miles away another woman prayed. *"God, show me your plans for us."* She had loved the Lord a long time and knew that God would use her somehow. She just didn't know how. Impatient, she begged, *"God, give me something to hang onto. Show me a picture. Show me what it is that I am waiting for. Show me where we will go. Show me what we will do. Then I can wait patiently."*

God loved this persistent woman. Talking to God was as natural as breathing to Grace. With a grateful heart she sang His praises. Self-centered, she whined and complained. Like a child she expected the miraculous. She prayed without ceasing. When she blamed Him for things gone wrong, He showed her truth and she gained understanding. Whatever the time or the season, she knew God was pleased to hear from her. Her confidence came from relationship with Him. Sure of an answer, she pushed and prodded.

Grace knew that a life spent serving God would involve excitement and adventure. She embraced the adventure, but had yet to count the cost. Trials and hardships can occur in the midst of adventure. Often they are the adventure. Grace wasn't ready for trials and hardship. None of us are. That's why we rely on God for guidance and protection. God knew this about

Grace, of course, but He loved her. He was willing to indulge her.

Grace settled back and waited. She understood that patience was key. God comforted her complaints and coddled her short-comings. He corrected false accusations with truth and wisdom. He had helped her to grow and learn about Him. This one thing she had learned well; God always rewards patience. She sat there expecting a vision, a picture of what God had planned for her life. Home alone, she had all afternoon. She was willing to wait as long as necessary.

She didn't wait long.

A picture of herself and her husband, Mark, opened up before her eyes. In it she was sitting high up on a wagon seat, driving the wagon across a wide golden plain. Mark walked beside the wagon.

"Wait! Wait! Where are the mountains? I know there have to be mountains."

Years before God had instructed Mark and Grace to go to the mountains. His plans for them had always included the mountains. Having grown up in the flatlands of New Jersey, this command to go to the mountains enchanted both Mark and Grace. Anticipation captivated their every thought. When? Where? How?

Where God guides, God provides. When opportunity arose, Mark and Grace took a deep breath and a step of faith. They settled into the mountains of Pennsylvania, and they loved every minute of it.

God chuckled at Grace's insistence on seeing the mountains. In fact, He'd waited for it. He is the one who gives us the desires of our hearts. He had instilled this love, this expectancy, of mountains in Grace's heart. The vision panned back away from the wagon on the plain and there, in the background, were tall beautiful, golden, treeless mountains – mirroring the color of the plain.

Grace pondered on this. She'd never imagined golden, treeless mountains. *"Where is this place?"*

Instantly she knew. *"Mongolia!"* Grace shouted in response to her own question. She took in a short breath and exhaled slowly. She'd long felt led to serve God in Mongolia.

"Beautiful mountains, Lord. Thank you so much. Oh please, show me more."

The vision zoomed back in on the cart. Mark was gathering children and putting them in the wagon. Mark and Grace had long been supporters of Holt International Children's Services. It seemed natural that they might ever work for Holt in some capacity. Working with orphans seemed like a plan that God would have for them.

At the time that God had instructed them to go to the mountains; He also told them that they would have many children. He'd phrased it oddly – *'more children than the married woman.'* This puzzled Grace.

Nonetheless, she knew their future involved children - many children - and mountains.

Young Christians, not unlike David's mother, Mark and Grace had looked toward themselves to fulfill God's plans. Instead of waiting on Him they took in foster children. Not being God's plan, it didn't work out so well. Mark and Grace learned that the Lord had His own timing and as they waited they grew, not only in patience, but in blessing as well. Over the years, Mark and Grace raised up a prospering business and eight beautiful children. Still they waited, eager for the next step God had for them.

The picture of Mark gathering children and putting them in the wagon as she drove delighted Grace. She and Mark had worked together for years running the family business and raising the family God had given them. This vision of them - in the mountains, working together, gathering children, seemed perfect.

A sudden revelation rocked Grace out of her euphoria. She realized that in this vision, she and Mark didn't work together. This was his job. She was only on the wagon to help him for a season. How could that be? They'd always worked together. If this wasn't her job, then what did she do?

Another revelation rocked Grace. She realized that she taught English while Mark gathered the children. This was summer. She was off from school. She had spent the summer helping Mark, but she must soon return to school. Sitting on the wagon, Grace struggled with her emotions. She wasn't sure she wanted to return to school. She wanted to stay with

Mark. She loved being near him. She loved working with him. She loved the children. They shouldn't be separated. Why would God do this?

An intense feeling washed over Grace. She remembered how much she loved teaching. She loved the students. She loved being in charge. She loved everything about it......

A cold wind blew in from the mountains, interrupting her thoughts. It reminded her that summer would soon be over. Grace would have to make a choice – return to school or stay with the wagon. She continued to struggle to make a decision. It overwhelmed her. She couldn't give up teaching. That would be too hard. But she couldn't leave Mark and the children either.

"I still have time," Grace consoled herself, *"Summer isn't over."* She remained perched on the wagon. *"I'll make a choice later."*

The sound of Mark's voice calling from the side of the wagon interrupted her thoughts. *"Grace, Grace..."*

Turning, she answered....... *"Yes?"*

Mark was standing there holding an infant. A stoic young boy stood by his side.

"Don't those children go onto the wagon?" Grace's heart raced. She knew something was special about these children. Her heart leapt to her throat. Could it possibly be.........?

"These are the children I'm giving you."

Grace held her breath. He'd read her heart. He knew how much she'd wanted another child. Every day she had scanned the faces of the children they gathered into the wagon. Every day she had wondered, *"Could this child be mine?"*

Till now, the answer had been a resolute, *"No."*

Grace and Mark had eight children - four biological and four adopted. Embracing each new child with the same intense delight, age had never diminished Grace's maternal desire. Her heart ached to hold a small child in her arms as much now as it had when her first was born.

Adoption is a Christian concept. The Bible teaches us to love one another. It teaches us to treat each other as we would like to be treated. The Bible is clear. God is Creator of all mankind. He holds no favorites. He loves us all the same. We are to do likewise.

God chose to make Himself known through the Hebrew nation. It is through the Jews that our salvation comes. Jesus was a Jew, a man of dark hair and brown skin. Christianity springs from the Middle East – not America or Europe. We who are Christian are adopted into the family of God.

Not surprisingly, many things exist in the Bible that Westerners, not familiar with Eastern custom and tradition, fail to see. For example, when looking for a room in which to celebrate Passover, Jesus tells his disciples to follow the man carrying the water. A

Westerner shakes his head and wonders, *"Which man carrying the water will lead them to the upper room?"* A Middle Easterner knows that men don't carry water. A man, carrying water, is a rare sight. An Eastern mind easily envisions Biblical details unfathomable to the Western mindset.

While Christianity was birthed in the Middle East and is comprehensible to the Eastern mind, adoption is not. Confucius, Buddha and Allah all taught that only flesh of your flesh is acceptable. In many societies an illegitimate child is unacceptable. The abandoned or orphaned children are considered cursed. They hold a stigma of shame. Who would embrace this unwanted burden?

God, our Heavenly Father, does. Unwanted children hold a special place in His heart. He commands his people to care for widows and orphans and poor migrants as well as for those who preach and teach his word. To Him, a prophet of God holds no more importance than an illegitimate child.

Adoption starts with the love of God for all people. With this love He offers His salvation to the Gentiles. In the spirit of adoption, He accepts as His own all who choose His son, Jesus. Adopted, we are brought into the family of God with all the rights and privileges of sonship. We are then called to extend that same love to all. Adoption encapsulates the grace, the mercy, and the kindness of a loving God to an unwanted stranger.

That stranger is us.

CHAPTER V

The Vision Continues

Grace watched Mark hand the baby to her as she sat on the wagon. Gazing down on this newborn child, she nestled it in her arms. Their eyes locked. Grace knew somehow that this child was a girl. The baby in her arms knew no other mother. Looking at Grace with adoration, her eyes spoke. *"I love you, I love you. I love you."* With rapt attention neither broke the gaze. The bond was instantaneous. Grace never wanted to look away again. She wanted to memorize every detail of this beautiful baby.

A prodding thought broke through her reverie. *"There's another child."* The young boy remained standing stoically by Mark's side. Grace turned her attention to him. She knew she needed to take in every detail of this child as well. She would need to recognize him when she saw him next.

This boy was brown of skin but fair of hair. Neither child was endowed with the qualities she had imagined in a Mongolian child. This child's hair stood straight up from his head. Scared and unsure of himself, no shadow of a smile softened his demeanor. No tears were permitted. He just stood there. The word 'Stoic' was written across his small chest.

An enormous head accentuated by the biggest cheeks Grace had ever seen, added to his woebegone appearance. Questions bubbled through her mind, one upon another. *"Is there something wrong with him? Why is his head so big? Why is he just standing there? What is wrong with him?"*

Studying the boy intently, Grace had to ask, *"God, why is his head so big? Is there something wrong with him?"*

"No, it's just big."

Relieved, Grace accepted this answer and resumed studying the children. They both had light hair. The boy's hair was darker than the girl's, but still fair. Puzzled she looked closer. The baby's hair was the same color as her youngest daughter's. It was a bright, white blond color.

"How can this be?" Grace thought all Asian people had straight, black hair. She spoke out loud. *"How can these children be Mongolian?"*

No response came. Impatient, Grace pressed for an answer. *"How can they be so fair?"*

"You will see in time."

It wasn't the answer Grace was looking for, but the vision proceeded.

Grace continued to see herself perched on the wagon. Another cold wind blew through her light, summer clothes. Grace knew that her season was over. She had no winter clothing. Time was short. She needed to choose. Would she give up teaching to stay with the wagon?

Feeling restless, Grace fidgeted. The churning in the pit of her stomach grew till she could feel it rising up in her throat. What should she do? How could she give up teaching? She didn't want to. How could she leave the wagon? She didn't want that either. She sat frozen, unable to move, unable to make a decision.

Struggling with choices, Grace became aware again of the baby in her arms, of the small boy waiting for her on the ground. This she hadn't yet considered. The children entrusted to her required her attention. Grace now understood what she needed to do. She needed to get down off the wagon and take care of these children God had entrusted to her. Grace had no desire to quit teaching and no heart to leave Mark or the wagon, but she knew what God expected of her.

Grace watched herself struggle emotionally in the vision. She saw herself get down from the wagon. She watched as she cradled the baby and reached out for the young boy. Watching this vision, Grace experienced all the emotions that Grace on the wagon was feeling. She marveled that someday she would have to make this choice. It all seemed so impossible to her, sitting there in her comfortable, Pennsylvania home.

The vision hung there for an indeterminate amount of time before it slowly continued. A silver haired gentleman appeared on the horizon. He was slender of build, not at all tall and his silver hair was cropped short. Walking across the plain towards Mark and Grace, he radiated a kind and gentle spirit. Greeting them, he invited Mark and Grace to follow him.

"Come with me."

"Who are you?" Grace was unnerved.

"Follow me."

"Where are we going? What will we do?"

"We'll ride the Mongolian ponies across the Steppes. There is something I want to give you."

Grace shot Mark a questioning look. Mark nodded his willingness to go. They followed not knowing where they were going. Their route wound through velvety mountains and across large empty plains. For days they followed an unmarked path. Though beauty surrounded them, fear of losing their way filled Grace with concern. She pressed the gentleman with further questions. *"Who are you? Are you a missionary? Do you work for Holt? What do want to show us? Why are we here?"*

"No, I am not a missionary."

"Then what?"

As they come across the valley a long, low, gray, concrete building emerged from the plain. It appeared abandoned. Exploring the inside, Mark and Grace found dust and dirt covering everything. Beakers and old laboratory equipment lay broken on dirty counters.

"What is this place?" Grace thought to herself.

"What is this place?" she asked aloud.

"It looks like an old abandoned military installation." Answering herself, she wrinkled her nose at the thought. It wasn't quite what she had hoped for.

"I'm giving this all to you." The silver-haired gentleman gestured at the building and the land surrounding it.

"But what is it? Who are you? Why are you giving this to us? Is this yours? Are you a missionary? Are you retiring? Is this an orphanage?" Grace rattled off questions faster than answers could be returned.

"No I'm not retired." The gentleman's eyes twinkled. *"I am just giving this all to you."*

Grace wasn't sure she wanted it. It was dirty. It needed a lot of work. And why was this man giving this place to them. For an orphanage? Was this their future? An orphanage in the mountains. Children and mountains. Why not? But no answers were forthcoming.

"You will understand." The silver haired gentleman spoke with gentle assurance.

The vision ended leaving Grace confused. Her questions remained unresolved. This is the way of visions. Given a glimpse of the future, revelation commences at its own pace.

Visions tend to make sense piece by piece, bit by bit, and not necessarily in the order that you were shown. They are God's way of enticing us to seek after Him. Unanswered questions keep us knocking at His door. The desire for revelation draws us near to Him. A vision is God's invitation to spend more time with Him.

It would take years and years for Grace to begin to see this vision unfold. To this day it is still unfolding. Little by little, pieces fall into place. Each new revelation causes her to sit back and soak in the wonder of it all. Each piece of the vision revealed grows her faith and teaches her anew that God is always in control.

Is a vision from God available for everyone? The Bible tells us to ask and we will receive. The Bible says that we 'have not' because we 'ask not'. If you've committed your heart to Jesus and want to know His plan for your life, then ask Him. Keep asking Him. God is always looking for people who will spend time with Him.

CHAPTER VI

A Mother's Love

Excitement raced through Grace's veins. The vision had inflamed her imagination. Eager to share it, her thoughts turned toward Mark.

"Uh-oh......... Better to ask first," Grace closed her eyes, rethinking her first impulse.

Wisdom suggests we consult with God before sharing a vision. A vision or an insight meant for the receiver alone can be meaningless to others, deflating the spirit, casting doubt on an intimate moment shared with our Creator.

"Can I tell Mark about this?"

"Absolutely."

Grace told Mark everything the minute he walked in the door.

With charm and patience Mark listened as Grace told him about the vision. When she finished, he blew the whole thing off. He wasn't sure about visions. He'd never had one. He wondered if Grace's visions weren't the result of an overactive imagination. They were real to her, that much Mark understood. They weren't as meaningful to him. He found explanations for the things she saw. Pushing into God for revelation didn't come naturally for him at that time. He was too busy for this kind of stuff. He left visions to Grace. Grace, however, remained exuberant. Replaying it over and over in her mind, she pondered the things she hadn't understood.

The next day a brochure arrived in the mail from Holt International Children's Services. It featured the children's home that Holt had recently partnered with in Mongolia. To Grace's astonishment quite a number of the children in the pictures had fair hair. The first piece of the puzzle fell into place.

"Look at this! People in Mongolia don't all have dark hair. Fair-haired Mongolian children! Who'd have thought it? A vision yesterday and confirmation today. God is sooooo good!"

Grace danced a jig in the kitchen. She flew high all day. Waiting to show Mark the brochure as she envisioned his reaction, her excitement was contagious. Of this she was sure.

Mark rarely got excited. This brochure proved no exception. He agreed that the timing of the brochure's arrival was probably from God. He also agreed that it seemed to confirm the vision. Still, he had other things to do. As time went on Mark forgot about the vision. Grace, however, continued to hold the vision in her heart.

Years later Mark and Grace received a visitor from the Holt organization. A silver haired gentleman with a twinkle in his eye, he was there to raise interest, money and support for the work Holt was doing. They had a new project. A small group was planning to build a playground for the children at the infant sanitarium in Ulaan Baatar, Mongolia. The silver-haired gentleman asked if they'd be interested in joining the group. *"While we're there,"* he told them, *"we'll ride the Mongolian ponies across the Steppes to an old, abandoned military installation. It's been turned into a vacation resort."*

Grace's chin dropped: The silver haired gentleman? Mongolia? Mongolian ponies? Steppes? Old abandoned military installation? He seemed slightly different than the man in the vision, but everything else seemed right.

"Count us in!" Grace barely contained herself. Mark nodded in agreement. It was out of his hands. He understood by now that Mongolia held a piece of their destiny. A major commitment he wasn't sure of, but that wasn't what was demanded of them. A small step, this ten day trip, was manageable.

Thus the adventure began.

After the Holt representative left, Mark teased Grace, *"Should we start the adoption paperwork immediately or wait until after we meet these children?"* His eyes sparkled as he spoke. He knew by now that when God talked to Grace it was only a matter of time before God followed through. Mark didn't doubt for a minute that their family would be growing again in the immediate future.

....

David's mother had made a painful decision. Growing steadily weaker since the birth of her son, she watched her hopes and dreams disappear. There were good days, but not enough of them. The strength to take Gana out into the sunshine – the glorious Mongolian sunshine – eluded her. Daily she lay on her bed, too weak to care for her beloved child.

Gana himself grew weak and flaccid. Too sick to cry out, he often went hungry. He'd contracted Hepatitis B, Hepatitis C and Syphilis from his mother at birth. His newborn immune system never developed sufficiently to fight these diseases. Without resistance, these diseases attacked his body relentlessly.

Without sunshine for vitamin D or milk for calcium Gana developed rickets. His spine began to curve. His bones grew soft and weak. His large head was too heavy. He couldn't lift it like other infants his age. Gana never rolled over. He never sat up. He never began to crawl. He lay there in squalor and misery, his life ebbing alongside of his mother's. His days and nights unchanged inside the gher.

By October Gana caught a cold. His weakened body couldn't shake it off. His mother held him when she could. She fed him what she could. When she felt well enough she had to work. On those occasions, she left him alone. Which was worse she couldn't say. Leaving him or watching him waste away, neither was a part of the life she'd envisioned.

Oh, how she loved this son of hers, this answer to prayer, this fulfillment of dreams, this child she'd so long awaited. There was but one thing she could not do. She could not watch him die. She would give him up and trust God before she would do that. Trusting in herself had failed miserably. No options remained. She could trust in God or watch Gana die.

When the cold November winds began to blow she knew her time with Gana was over. She wrapped him in the best piece of cloth she had. It wasn't much more than a rag by most standards. She laid him in a basket and carried him into town. The note she pinned to the blanket stated his full name and date of birth. He was born on Children's Day. People should know that. He was named Ganerdene Erdene Ochir, Gana for short. He was a strong beautiful treasure. Whoever found him should know that also.

Feeling conspicuous in the nicer part of town David's mother chose an apartment complex in a seedier section. More familiar with this part of town, she could move about unnoticed. Though old and dilapidated the building housed a variety of families. She prayed that a good one would find her boy and care for him.

David's mother smuggled her bundle into the apartment building. She left the basket in a warm corner of the stairwell. She never looked back. Walking away, the tears pent up from years of defeat rolled down her face. Two thoughts consoled her. If Anna spoke truth, she'd see Gana again in heaven. If God answered prayer, that wouldn't be for a long time.

David's mother was prepared to suffer the consequences for the choices she had made. Anna had explained that if we choose to smoke, we choose to destroy our lungs. If we choose to drink alcohol to excess then we choose to destroy our liver. If we choose to sell our bodies then we choose to be exposed to every kind of disease.

While this can be true for the unrepentant sinner, or the unrepentant believer, or even the unbelieving believer, those who stand on His Word believe that God forgives our behaviors and washes away our sin. He changes our lives. He heals us. He delivers us from all that would hold us captive. He paid the price to do just that. He died to set us free. Free from sickness, from infirmity, from disease, from pain, from anything that would bind us to the enemy. He set us free to live our lives here on earth walking in all His promises. Yet often enough, we don't receive or stand on His promises. We face the consequences of our own actions without taking His actions into account. Even then, He never leaves us comfortless.

David's mother reckoned she'd earned her consequences. With Gana gone she had nothing left to live for. She never asked God to heal her. She only asked for forgiveness. But she did ask God to both heal and forgive her son. Gana was blameless in this. If God were real, she reckoned, Gana could be completely healed; this especially, if she asked nothing for herself.

God can and does heal. It is His heart's desire that we all are healed. Often healing is a miracle. Just as often healing can be a slow process. The end result is the same. David's mother didn't ask for a miracle. She asked for Gana's healing. Since Gana's sickness was the direct result of her poor choices, she asked for forgiveness for them. It is in forgiveness that healing comes. David's mother was right to pray. God answers prayer. She was right to ask forgiveness. She was right to ask for healing. She was right to trust Gana to Jesus.

Jesus never left or abandoned David's mother. One day He gently removed her from sickness and pain, sorrow and misery. He brought her to live with Him in heaven, to a place He had prepared for her. There, God embraced her. He explained just how much He loved her and Gana. He promised that He would honor her faith and her prayers. He assured her that she would see her Gana again. Much to her delight, it would not be soon. All fear dissolved. Darkness fled. Tears of gratitude streamed down her face. David's mother broke and fell into her Savior's arms. She was finally home.

CHAPTER VII

Who Will Love This Child?

In the dimly lit hallway of that dark, dirty apartment building Gana was found. Several people had passed by, unaware of the child hidden in the dark recess under the stairs. After hours without food or liquid he let out a pitiful cry. A neighbor investigated the unusual sound.

What they found was nothing short of disgusting. Sickness and disease exploded from every orifice of David's body. Puss oozed from his eyes, his ears, his nose, his mouth, from his private parts. This baby was more dead than alive. This was a child no one wanted to touch – let alone wanted. So beloved in the eyes of his mother, he repulsed the eyes of others.

Taken to the infant sanitarium in Ulaan Baatar, Gana was left for others to deal with. The neighbor walked away and never came back to see if Gana had lived or died. He didn't care. He didn't want to care. Life, he knew, was hard enough without taking on other people's trouble.

God cared however, and He had a plan. He placed people in Gana's life that would love him. Tsetseg, the nurse at the sanitarium cared deeply for all the children under her charge. She hated loosing even one child. Though she doubted that Gana would live, she fought for him. She insisted that Gana be washed and fed and given his medicine.

A nanny at the sanitarium with a heart for disabled children took special care of Gana. She took him under her wing, massaging his emaciated limbs and feeding him when he refused to eat. *"Here is a child worth saving,"* she repeated to all who would listen.

If Tsetseg and the nanny found Gana worth saving, the doctors disagreed. At five months of age Gana had never lifted his head. His emaciated body emphasized the fact that his head was too large. Hydrocephalus, water on the brain, was diagnosed. If Gana lived he would be mentally slow, maybe retarded. It was better, they agreed, to let this child die than burden society.

Like his mother in so many ways, when things looked their worst Gana grew stronger. He clung to the life giving hope of his caretakers. A long slow process, his healing took root. Food, medicine and caretakers all joined together to breathe new life into him. His eyes missed nothing. His ears distinguished voices. He learned to make new sounds. Then the unthinkable happened. Lying on the mat with the other children, Gana's body began to convulse. It was a seizure; a stroke. How much more could this tiny body take?

It was another seizure; another stroke. *"Just see that he is made comfortable until he dies."* Tsetseg had given up hope. *"That is the best we can do for this child."* The staff agreed.

But Gana did not agree. He clung tenaciously to life. Everyday he grew a little stronger. One day he rolled over. Physically months behind his peers, he finally did it. He kept on doing it. His infectious smile lit up the room. The staff marveled at his progress.

Gana learned to push himself up and to crawl. He learned to sit up. Every milestone well behind his peers, but once accomplished, was never forgotten. Gana was growing up. He was catching up. He was watching and imitating the things he saw around him.

"He's not so slow." Tsetseg passed her observation on to Tsemble, the social worker. She was the one who recommended children to forever families.

"No, he isn't! We can find a home for him." The nanny beamed with pride.

Tsemble agreed. *"No, he doesn't seem slow at all. He is behind, but he's catching up. He's getting well. There is something special about him. Maybe we can find him a home."*

Gana possessed an insatiable appetite to know what was going on around him. More than curious, Gana was nosey. Exploring everything, leaving nothing untouched, he learned all he could learn. To catch up to the other children was all that he desired.

By the end of his second year, Gana could walk. He was unsteady, of course. His large head toppled him if he leaned too far in one direction or the other. Luckily his head was hard. It survived more than the average number of childhood tumbles.

By the time he was two and a half, David was putting two or three words together and forming simple sentences. At this age the average toddler is rattling on incessantly. The average toddler has had years of people talking to him and teaching him new words. Children raised in a children's home don't have that luxury. The nannies are busy changing diapers and washing clothes, feeding the children and potty training them. They don't take the time to talk to the children under their care – except to tell them to eat or be quiet. They don't sing to them or rock them or whisper in their ears. The children are not encouraged to talk. They understand commands, but are rarely verbal. Everything David could speak he had learned by listening to the nannies. He was ahead of his peers in the sanatorium.

"The brightest boy in the nursery," the nannies all agreed.

Gana was bright. He was nosey. He loved to talk. Wherever trouble brewed, there was Gana – irresistibly drawn in. If anyone woke up in the night - Gana watched to see what they would do. If anyone fought over a toy – Gana knew who started it. If anyone threw away food – Gana saw who it was. If the nannies needed information, they just asked Gana. And he told.

"A real tattletale," the nannies all laughed; *"And a very big help."*

....

Some children are left at the sanitarium till their parents can get their lives together. Out of work or sick, they come and visit their children. They make a plan to bring them home. Orphaned, some children wait till relatives can be found to take them home. Perfect and healthy, some children are available for adoption. If both parents legally render their custodial rights, a child can be adopted. An abandoned child is different. A search is required. Advertisements placed in the newspaper seek parents or relatives to claim this child. If no one comes forward, after six months that child becomes available for adoption.

This was Gana's case. The sanitarium had searched for David's mother but she never came forward. She was at home with the Lord. Gana became available for adoption.

Available doesn't mean adoptable. As bright and as handsome as David had become his health remained a recipe for disaster. No one wanted this sickly child. No one in their right mind would take on a child with so many health problems.

At the same time that Gana arrived at the sanitarium three other infants also arrived. Within a short time they became inseparable. Other children came and went of course, but these four closed their ranks to the others. Their years together created an unspoken bond.

When the children turned one, they moved together from the infant room to the toddler room. They ate together. They slept together. They potty trained together. When one fell the others pulled him up. The next year they moved again to the two year old room. Together they formed a protective barrier against the world.

In the sanitarium all the children are told that one day their forever parents will come for them. They must wait and be patient. True enough, one by one forever parents arrived for each of Gana's friends. The foursome became a threesome, then a twosome. One bright day a car arrived with another forever family. Waving goodbye the twosome became one. Though Gana's eyes glistened as he watched the car pull away, he didn't cry. He never cried. Crying never changed anything.

Gana now waited alone for his forever family.

With each new parting Gana's demeanor changed. His shoulders drooped a little more. His head hung lower. *"When will my forever family come?"*

"Soon. Soon." The nannies repeated themselves, exchanging glances.

No one ever came.

Gana suspected a lie. Other children were sent away when they turned three. They never returned. *"The State Children's Home,"* the nannies whispered when they looked at Gana. *"Soon."* The words caused a chill to run down his spine. Fear, doubt and unbelief found their foothold. His 'forever' parents would never find him there.

He was right.

On June 1st of 2002, Gana would be three. It would be his turn to leave the comfort of the Infant Sanitarium. The Children's Home meant institutionalization till the age of sixteen. It was the end of the road for a child like Gana with no family to come for him. Adoption opportunities no longer exist at the State Home. After sixteen it's the army or the streets.

"No," the nannies fretted.

"It's not good for a child." Tsemble was worried. *"We need more time."* She took pictures of Gana and put them in an adoption magazine, hoping to find a forever family.

"When will my forever family come?" Gana's voice wavered.

"Soon." The nannies reassured Gana, but they no longer believed it themselves.

Gana felt their unbelief down to the bottom of his two year old soul. He no longer believed it either. *"No. I will never have a forever family."* His head drooped lower. His shoulders sagged further still.

"Please Lord, Please take care of my child," David's mother begged from heaven.

We here on earth, cannot pray to our ancestors for help. They are dead. They cannot hear us. They cannot see us. They cannot come back down to earth. They can neither help nor hurt us. They can do nothing for us. They possess no special powers. Those who are alive in heaven with Jesus cannot hear our prayers either, but they know who can. It is Jesus that sees all things and hears all things and knows all things.

Those alive in Christ are in the presence of God. They can talk to Him directly. The Bible tells us that Jesus lives to make intercession for us. That means that He lives to pray for us – to intercede – to talk to God for us. Why, when we are in heaven, would we not follow His example?

This is exactly what David's mother did. She called on the God who loved her so much to remember His promise to watch over her son. God, being an honorable God, had never forgotten His promise. Reaching out, He rested His hand on her shoulder. Reassured, she rested her head on His shoulder.

He'd planned it all out from the beginning of time. He was prepared to act on her prayer the first second she prayed. God being an honorable God had to wait for that prayer. He cannot come into a heart uninvited. He cannot come into a home where He is not called upon. He cannot answer an unspoken prayer. Prayer changes things because prayer gives an honorable God permission to act on our behalf.

A young woman had turned to God in her hour of need. Her prayer had been heard. The promise of God had been made and His promises cannot be broken.

God smiled as He consoled David's mother. Her prayer was being answered as they spoke. Grace and Mark were packing their bags. They were going to Mongolia to help build a playground at the Infant Sanitarium. They were going to meet the child God had shown them in a vision years ago. David's mother had whispered her thanks to God for a son. She had asked for His protection over him. Set in motion the moment she prayed, the plan was unfolding.

God always has a plan. His plans are for good and not for evil. His plans are for a future and a hope for those who love Him. His plans are always released with prayer and thanksgiving.

CHAPTER VIII

There is Hope

It was a warm spring day in the Poconos. Grace glowed with anticipation. Was this it? Would they find God's purpose for them in Mongolia? Would they see the children from the vision? Wanting to recognize the children, Grace pictured them over and over again in her mind. Packing was of little consequence. Grace's mind soared. She knew that to release God's plans she needed to be in agreement with them, with Him. Grace was more than 'in agreement'. She was, as usual, impatient.

In May of 2002, Mark and Grace flew to San Francisco. They met up with the rest of the group a few days later and flew on to Beijing. In Beijing, the group rested before going on to Mongolia. Every day hung suspended in time, wasted time in Grace's mind, an unwelcome delay. She had only one desire. She wanted to see the children God had shown her. China was awesome. It was exotic. It was wonderful. However, it was God's plan that drew her. It was God's plan that held her in suspense.

Arriving in Ulaan Baatar, they found it to be everything they had been told. The sun shone brightly, through air choked with coal smoke. An azure sky framed mountains dusted with gray snow. No green grass was seen in the city. No color was seen at all.

Cold, gray, Communist era architecture dominated the skyline. Trash littered the streets where dirty children and old women begged. Though now a democracy, the Communist Party yet ruled. Mongolia was in those days, a study in contradictory expectations.

Food bewildered Western thinkers as well. Potatoes were considered vegetables. Cabbage, the closest thing to a salad that could be found, was served raw for breakfast. Neither fresh fruit nor vegetables were to be found – anywhere – in 2002. The few international restaurants in the city served food that tasted the same, regardless of the establishment or the dish chosen.

"Could you actually consider living here?" Jay expressed doubt.

"Yes, we could." Mark sounded surprisingly upbeat. When God gives you a vision, you start to see things through His eyes. It's new and exciting. With God, it's an adventure.

"Are you a Christian?" Grace questioned Hoyt, the driver.

"No. I've read the Bible through three times and I don't understand it. Mongolians don't believe in God. We are atheist."

"Are you a Christian?" Mark asked their translator.

"No, I've been to the new Mormon Church three times and I don't understand it. Mongolians are atheist." The translator shrugged her shoulders.

"If they've read through the Bible three times and have gone back to church three times, they are seeking answers. They may be atheist, but they are seeking after truth. They need someone to make it clear." Mark saw through God's eyes. His perspective was God's perspective. Possibilities danced in his eyes.

Grace nodded in agreement.

"The Mongolian people are so friendly. They always smile at you. When you smile at them, they always smile back. I feel comfortable here." Mark was seeing past the ten day trip. His vision had begun to expand.

Grace agreed. Making mental notes, she began to count the cost. *"Pollution – awful in winter. Television – BBC, but at least it's in English. People – good. Mountains – good. Food – not so good. Housing? Hmmmm??"*

The newly finished Ghengis Khan Hotel, the nicest place in town at that time, offered comfortable accommodations. *"What about other housing? Affordable housing?"* Grace looked up and down the streets.

"I'm sure those apartments are finished off nicely on the inside," Ron nodded toward the apartments opposite the hotel. Looking at the gray, dingy buildings, Grace wasn't convinced.

The next day the group toured the Infant Sanitarium before settling down to work on the playground. While the building project held the attention of the men, the ladies were captivated by the babies. They gave them English names. They picked favorites.

Asking the nannies to heat some water, they bathed each tiny child. They hugged the babies. They held them. They cuddled them. They rocked them. The babies loved the attention. They thrived on it. They expected it. They demanded it. Each night after the ladies left, the room was filled with soulful cries of babies wanting more. Doing their chores to a chorus of crying babies, the nannies longed for the ladies to go home permanently and leave them to their quiet routine.

Grace scrutinized each baby. None matched the one she had seen in her vision. No children in the one year old room matched either. Wandering up the stairs to the two year old room, Grace looked around. Inhaling sharply, she stepped back. Here, among the other children, was the child she had seen in the vision years earlier. God had shown Grace what David would look like years before she found him. The thought astounded Grace. She stood there, her mouth gaped open.

Small for his age, Gana would be three years old in less than a month. His light brown hair stuck straight up in the back. His head was large. As his big brown eyes beheld Grace and he stopped playing with the other children. Sensing the unknown, he stood still, neither looking at Grace nor looking away. Shy and scared, unsure of himself, he showed no emotion.

'*Stoic,*' Grace saw the word written across his chest.

"Can I take that little boy outside with me to see the playground and to meet Mark?" Grace held her breath.

"Which one?" The nannies frustration showed.

"That one there with the big head. Not that one. That one!!"

"Ahhhh, Gana."

The nannies hesitated. Did they need to stop what they were doing to dress this child for the cold Mongolian air? He would be off his schedule. He needed to take a nap when they all took their naps. Then there was potty time. Throw one child off his routine and they all fussed.

Grace sought an ally. Tsemble proved worthy of the challenge. She convinced the nannies that after naptime and potty time Grace could come back. *"The fresh air will do him good."*

The nannies grumbled amongst themselves.

On the playground, Paul recognized Gana immediately. A Holt employee, he came in and out of Mongolia regularly. Gana had caught his eye. *"He's my favorite! He's so friendly and playful. He's a happy child."*

"No, he's not. He's quiet and shy. He wants to cry, but he won't. He's serious. He's stoic. Just look at him."

Everyone turned to look at Gana. Confused, he stood there with a blank look on his small face. He'd never been separated from the group. He'd never been taken anywhere alone. He wondered if they were taking him to the Children's Home. He'd heard the nannies whispering. They said it would be his turn soon. They said it wouldn't be a good thing.

Gana was scared. He had been lonely when his friends had left one by one, but there were other children in the sanitarium. This was different. He didn't recognize these people. He couldn't understand what they were saying. He didn't know what was going to happen next. He stared straight ahead. The one thing he knew was that he wouldn't cry. The nannies had told him not to. He stood his ground and held back the tears.

"I have never seen him like this. He's just a little scared. He'll loosen up in a while." This wasn't the child that Paul knew. He patted Gana on the head.

Tsemble agreed. *"Gana is a happy boy, full of life and mischief. And he is talkative. He's our tattletale. He tells us everything."*

Yet, there he stood. Small and solemn, he spoke not a word.

Grace pondered this in her heart.

Gana never did loosen up. Not that day. Not the next; or the next; or the next. Grace played with him. She gave him an apple. She held him and whispered sweet, gentle words in his ear. She promised to be his forever family. She promised to come back and get him soon.

Day after day Grace came back to him. She brought him outside. He stood one step behind her as she painted the swings, never smiling. She pushed him on the swings. She slid with him down the slide. She helped him climb onto the jungle gym. She gave him another apple. Not one smile broke his demeanor.

Gana never became that happy, chatty little boy that Tsemble and Paul and the nannies knew. Neither did he ever cry or throw a temper tantrum. He remained that silent, stoic little boy that Grace had seen in her vision.

Grace knew in her heart that this was from God. Contrary to Gana's natural behavior and personality he remained silent. Every day it became clearer to Grace that this was the child God was giving them. God was showing them the boy from the vision, and his name was Gana.

"Is Gana available for adoption?" Grace worked up the nerve up to ask Tsemble about him.

"Yes, he is. But we don't do that."

"Don't do what?"

"We do not allow people to come here and choose children. We cannot do that. We cannot promise him to you. If someone else has all their paperwork and they want him, then we will give him to them. We cannot tell a waiting couple that we have promised him to someone else. We don't know that you will come back for him. We cannot turn down approved parents."

Grace nodded enthusiastically. The only thing she heard was that Gana was available. Her smile gave her away.

"*Do you understand?*"

"*Yes. If I can get all my paperwork in before anyone else, then can I have him?*"

"*No, we cannot promise you anything. Gana will be three soon. He will be moved to the Children's Home. Then no one can adopt him. Do you understand? You cannot just come here and pick a child.*"

"*Yes, I understand.*" Grace's mind raced ahead through the adoption process.

"*So, go home. If you wish to adopt a child then go through the adoption paperwork and apply. Do you understand that you will probably not get Gana?*"

"*Yes. I understand.*" Grace bit her tongue. She tried not to smile. Gana was available. He was hers. Her heart raced.

"*Do you still think you that you will get this particular child?*"

"*Yes!*" Unable to hold back a grin, Grace beamed. "*I know I will get him.*"

The Infant Sanitarium may not be able to promise a child to you, but God can. The promises of God are unbreakable. Grace knew her God well enough to know this. She flew home with praise on her lips and pictures of Gana in her pocket.

Tsemble smiled to herself when the group departed. "*I think Gana has found his forever family,*" she informed the nannies.

The nannies informed Gana. *"Gana, your forever family will come one day and get you."*

Gana already knew this. Looking up, his eyes met theirs. With a mature confidence beyond his years he answered them. *"Now I believe my forever family will come."* No footholds remained. Fear, doubt, and unbelief had disappeared. Gana's two year old heart was at rest.

Tears filled the nannies' eyes. Ten days remained before Gana's third birthday and his departure for the Children's Home. *"There must be a God,"* they agreed, *"and He talks to Gana."*

CHAPTER IX

Decisions

Grace and Mark flew directly home. They embraced each child anxiously awaiting their return. Hugs and kisses came first. Then, eager to share, each child filled them in on all that had happened in their absence. The cacophony rose and ebbed as one child spoke over the other. Laughter ensued, filling in any possible moments of silence. It was good to be home, surrounded by the bubbling over of family. There was now, however, a new hole cut into in their hearts. A child was missing. Awaiting the bustle to subside, Grace slowly pulled out the picture she had carried with her. She showed her children a small sad child that no one wanted. *"This is Gana. He needs a home."*

It was roundly agreed amongst the siblings. *"Let's get him! Let's get him!"*

Everyone agreed, that is, except Honorah. The baby of the family for six years desired no competition for attention. *"I'm the baby. No new children!"* Honorah stamped her foot and stood her ground.

"You're six years old. You are not a baby any longer."

"I'm the youngest! We don't need new children."

"No one wants him. He's getting too old to be adopted. If we don't get him then no one will. He will never have a family."

"Then we need to get him," Honorah bowed her head and spoke softly, reluctantly. She would, from time to time regret this decision, but it was now unanimous. The race was on to bring Gana home.

As quickly as humanly possible Mark and Grace filed for foreign adoption. A mountain of paperwork challenged them daily: three separate physicals – each, an FBI background check, local police checks, an adoption study, a home study, finger print checks, pediatrician's reference, job references, financial checks, child abuse clearances. All required paperwork - filled out in triplicate.

With a six month backlog of adoption studies on its calendar, the local adoption agency hired a new social worker. She came out within a week. Luck ...... or God? For Grace no such question arose. She knew God's handiwork when she saw it.

In record time Grace and Mark sent their paperwork to Holt. By September they were ready to be assigned a country. Too old to be considered elsewhere, the only country that would accept them was Mongolia. *"Another God thing!!"* Spirits soaring, Grace was all in.

Then the trials commenced.

A call came in from Holt. *"We cannot accept your application. You are too old for any other country than Mongolia and Mongolia is backlogged. We cannot even put you on the waiting list."*

"God, did I get this all wrong? Did I misunderstand everything?" Grace's joy came crashing down from heavenly heights to earthly realities. "I know He has a plan, but what could it be?"

"OK. I understand." Grace hung her head. She didn't understand. She was crushed.

"All things work together for good. All things work together for good. All things work together for good." Grace chose God's words over doubt.

"However," the voice on the other end of the line continued, *"I've noticed that the child you specifically wish to adopt has some physical problems. If you are willing to take a child with some physical problems then we can jump you to the front of the line. You don't even need to go on the waiting list. Waiting children, children with disabilities, are a priority."*

Grace rose from her seat. Her heart beat rapidly. She couldn't believe what she'd just heard. "No waiting list. Front of the line. Priority. God did have a plan!"

Suddenly her spirits sank as quickly as they had soared. "What physical problems?"

"A laundry list of problems really." With each new physical problem listed Grace's heart sunk a little further. *"Gana had syphilis. It went undiagnosed till he was about eighteen months old. We feel that the seizures he suffered were a result of the syphilis. The*

seizures induced at least two strokes. Penicillin has cured the syphilis and he hasn't had any more seizures since that time. We can't guarantee that he'll never have another one. We just don't know what is wrong. And he seems to be a little weak on his left side."

"One – syphilis. Two - seizures. Three – strokes." Grace counted quietly to herself. *"But God can heal that."* Grace encouraged herself as her heart broke over this beautiful child she now counted as her own. *"And this is His plan. We can handle that."*

"Is that all?"

"Actually no, he has been diagnosed with both Hepatitis C and Hepatitis B."

"Four – Hepatitis C. Five – Hepatitis B." Grace continued to count.

"And hydrocephalous."

"Six – hydrocephalous."

"And Ricketts. And curvature of the spine."

"Seven – Ricketts. Eight – Curvature of the spine."

Grace waited quietly to see if there were more. Could there possibly be more? How sick could a child be and still live? Grace sat stunned.

"I know you can't make this decision right now. I can send you Ganerdene's portfolio. You can take it to your pediatrician or a specialist and get some

advice about the viability of adopting a child with this many conditions. I know you'll need to talk it over with your husband."

"Yes. Send the portfolio. We'll get advice. We'll get back to you." Stunned Grace hung up the phone.

There the story might have ended had God not given a vision of a small Mongolian boy to an impatient woman and her husband from Pennsylvania. Had not this couple loved and trusted God the story would be done. Had they not gone to Mongolia and seen this child and held him in their arms and called him their own, it would be over.

No one in their right mind would have taken on a child with that many problems. No one in their right mind would travel halfway around the world to bring that child home. No one with eight beautiful, healthy children and a business to run would add these problems to their life. No one in their right mind would even consider this.

Mark and Grace weren't in their right minds. They had put on the mind of Christ. They were seeing this child with the love of God. They didn't know if it was their purpose to bring Gana home to help him die, or to bring him back to life. What they did know was that this was God's plan, and where God guides – God provides. God had guided them to Gana. God would provide them with whatever Gana needed.

They knew they didn't need to embrace God's plan. No one would blame them. God himself might not even blame them. How many times do we choose not to follow God's plan for our lives? How many times do we ignore that nudge He gives us? God still loves us. The only thing we lose by not following God's plan is the blessing that comes with it.

"How can taking on a child with this many problems be a blessing?" Grace wasn't sure she wanted to watch a child die, to watch her child die.

"Maybe we're the blessing for Gana," Mark suggested quietly.

They took the portfolio to specialists. *"Forget this child. He's lucky to still be alive. He won't live much longer."* The prognosis wasn't good.

"This is what they call a 'throw away' child. Even if he does live he will be mentally retarded. You will spend the rest of your lives becoming intimately acquainted with his special education teachers. It will be better if he died. He will be a liability for you all your lives."

No one offered encouragement.

"Hepatitis B is bad. Hepatitis C is worse. And the combination is deadly. No one survives both. You would be bringing him home to watch him die. And you would be exposing your whole family to deadly diseases." This doctor, a personal friend, was more sympathetic.

"The syphilis has been taken care of. One down," Grace countered. *"Ricketts can be taken care of with sunshine and vitamin D. Two down. And there have been no more seizures. Three down. And there seems*

to be no real signs of damage from the strokes. Four down. We're halfway there."

"We've dealt with Hepatitis B before. We can deal with that. Five down. The curvature of the spine isn't even noticeable. We saw him. With Vitamin D and the end of Ricketts it might not get worse. Six down."

"The hydrocephalous and the Hepatitis C? And long term effects of untreated syphilis?" The doctor pressed her point.

"I saw him. He has a big head, a huge head, but it is not hydrocephalic. In fact the nannies said he was the brightest child there."

"The brightest child in an institution does not make him a bright child."

"No! I've seen him. He's not retarded. He's just how God showed him to me."

As Grace thought things through, her determination grew. "Didn't I see a boy with a big head? Didn't I ask God why his head was so big? And what was it God said to me? He said it was just big. That was God telling me not to worry about it. He just has a big head."

"He's not hydrocephalic. We've seen him. That is a misdiagnosis." Grace stood emphatically on the word of God. God had said that it was just big. Grace refused to worry about it. "Seven down."

"The Hepatitis C, the combination of Hep B and Hep C, and the long term effects of syphilis?" The doctor pursued her line of thinking. *"Even that is much too much. Do you want to bring that into your family?"*

"If the hydrocephalus is a misdiagnosis, then the Hep C can be a misdiagnosis." Grace was stronger with every thought that crossed her mind. *"Then there will be no combination of Hep C and Hep B. God can take care of the long term effects of syphilis."* Grace was triumphant. *"Eight down."*

"You are hoping for a misdiagnosis." Grace's friend rebuked her. *"That doesn't make it true. He has been tested several times. He shows positive for Hep B and Hep C."*

"But isn't there a chance for a false positive?" The tone in Grace's voice pleaded for the answer to be 'yes'.

"Yes." Dr. Baily paused. She didn't want to give Grace any encouragement at all. *"It's possible. But it's not probable."*

Looking up at Grace and Mark, she saw the foolish look of hope on their faces. As strongly as she could, she admonished them. *"You may be making the biggest mistake of your lives. You may regret this forever."*

"Eight down," Grace sighed. *"We can do this."*

When they arrived home that day they discussed the matter. Hope rose and crashed and rose again. One minute truth lit their path. The next minute cold gray facts pushed in. Facts have a way of distorting the truth. Gana carried deadly diseases. That fact remained. Yet facts can change. The truth does not. God is our healer. This truth prevails against any fact.

Mark and Grace were slow to grasp the truth. *"The biggest adventure. The biggest mistake. Which could it be?"* They prayed. They cried. They wavered. *"God, if this is you, please let us know."*

Mark struggled to put it all together. *"How much more can he let us know? We had the vision. We saw this child with our own eyes. We fell in love with him. God answered our question before we knew it was a problem. His head is just big. God is a healer. We just need faith."*

"If we don't trust God and step out in faith, then we will never see any more than this. If we are faithful in the small things then He will trust us to be faithful in the bigger things. He is testing us to see if we will follow Him. We need to test God and see how far He will take us."

"Grace, we are going on an adventure with God. How can that be a bad thing?"

As the light of truth dawned on Grace and Mark they realized they'd be foolish not to embrace what God had given them.

Days later, while the warm September breezes blew gently through the trees, they called Holt. They called before they could change their minds again. *"We'll take him,"* was all they said. They weren't sure how this would turn out.

They made their choice, not in trepidation and fear of God. They did not fear God. They loved God and desired to follow Him. They made their choice in love and faith. However, they did not make their choice in joy and exaltation. They knew that much heartache and sorrow could lie before them.

God smiled in heaven. He knew that Mark and Grace would make this choice. Together they worked well for the Lord. When one was down or unsure, the other was an encourager. They lifted each other up. They gained strength from one another. God knew they would work through this.

"They'll take Gana." God leaned over and whispered to David's mother. He wiped away her tears. Both of these things are promised to us in the Bible, God's written word. He will take care of our children. He will wipe away all our tears in heaven.

"Gana will be taken care of." David's mother felt the peace that God promises each of us, warm her soul. She had been right to trust God. Gana would have a forever family that would give him all the love she had felt for him. God was a God of good promises.

Photo Album

**Brown Family – 2003
David in front.**

David with his Mongo-Lion

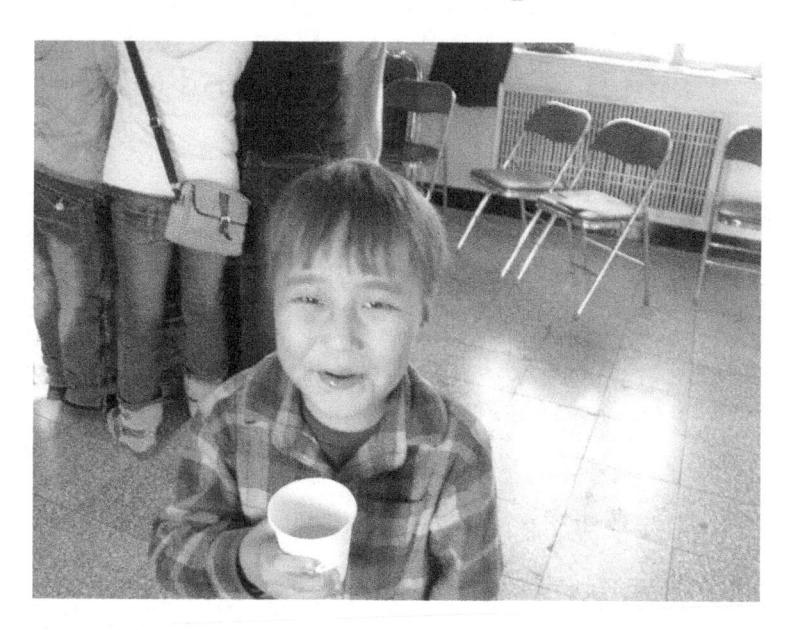

2006 Visiting China

**2007/2008 Living in Mongolia.
Visiting Kharhorum – Gengis Kahn's
Capitol with sister Sarah and MIU
students**

2010 – David and Honorah curl up on the couch.

David 2014

2018 – David's Graduation

David's hobby – capturing sunsets.

CHAPTER X

A Good, Strong Name

Gana's third birthday came and went, but he was spared from the Children's Home. He had a forever family and they were coming to get him. Soon. Very soon.

The nannies took him aside to train him. They showed him how to line up shoes in a row. They showed him how to throw trash into the trash can. They warned him to be helpful and respectful. *"Never fuss or cry. No one wants a crybaby."*

The gate to his soul cracked open. Fear crept back in.

Meanwhile, Mark and Grace and their family waited. The mountain of paperwork needed to be translated. Every word took precious time.

September ended brilliantly with a warm Indian summer. October blazed gloriously with the colors of autumn. Still they waited. November brought Thanksgiving. It also brought impatience. An empty place at the Thanksgiving table matched the emptiness in Grace's heart. Early December brought an end to the translation. The paperwork was nearly complete.

Once Gana was officially assigned to them, Mark and Grace had to choose a name for their new son to finalize the paperwork. Without an official, legal name there could be no passport or visa.

"He needs a strong name." Grace was insistent. "He has so much to face in his life. David was a man after God's own heart. John was the beloved of the Lord. Let's call him John David."

Mark's thoughts echoed Grace's. "God must have a wonderful plan for his life. I agree. He needs a strong name. It's John David."

So, Ganerdene Erdene Ochir, known as Gana, became John David Tinker, the beloved of God. It was a good strong name.

With the paperwork completed Graces impatience grew. She called Holt. "Can we travel to Mongolia and bring David home before Christmas?"

"No, by the time we set it up it may get into the Christmas holidays. Then we don't know how long it would take."

"That shouldn't be a problem. Mongolians don't celebrate Christmas."

"But we do and we are your support team. And so does the staff at the American Embassy. Everyone there takes the holidays off and goes home for two weeks."

"OK. Then January?" Grace wished it were already January.

"We already have two families scheduled to go in January and the Mongolian government only allows two adoptions per month."

"February?"

"It's very windy there in February. It's difficult to get into and out of Ulaan Baatar. Many pilots will not fly there in February. There's also the Lunar New Year. The whole country shuts down for several weeks. And we can't schedule anything because they still haven't decided when Lunar New Years will be."

"Oh my goodness! March?"

"Yes, that would be best. We can try to schedule it for then."

"You want us to wait three months? Can we take another look at December? We still have several weeks left. We can fly at a moments notice. Can you see if you can possibly schedule us for December?"

Patience was not Grace's best virtue. In her case, it was hardly a virtue at all. In her mind, David was theirs. All they had left to do was pick him up. Thanksgiving without her youngest son had been tolerable because the paperwork had not yet been done. Christmas would be a different story. Three more months? Impossible!

Tsemble had told them to call if they had a problem or question. They'd done that several times. The first time they confirmed that David was not mentally slow. Tsemble offered them assurance. *"All the nannies agree. David is very bright."*

The next time Mark called to check on the Hepatitis testing. *"Yes,"* Tsemble had said, *"the tests have been run several times and always with the same results."*

Mark called Tsemble at the sanitarium again in early December. *"Is it too late to schedule anything for December? Is it really unsafe to travel in February? What do you think?"*

"Oh yes, it is too late for December and we do have two families scheduled for January. However it is windier in March than in February. February is safe enough. I can call the office and tell them that. It's wonderful to know that new parents are eager to come and get their children. But February will have to be soon enough."

....

Cold and snowy, February 2003 finally arrived. Mark and Grace stood waiting at the departure gate for an interminable amount of time. Due to the weather, boarding had been delayed. Mark and Grace were uncomfortably warm. The deep cold of Mongolia required heavy clothes. Layered in warm clothing, perspiration trickled down their faces.

Anxious and pacing, Grace worried about the delay. Mark remained calm. He was always calm. Reaching out he stopped Grace from pacing. Drawing her close he held her still. His gaze compelled her to focus her attention on him. Finally he spoke. *"We don't have to do this you know. We can still walk away. We can never get on this plane. No one would blame us."*

Grace reacted nervously. She was overdressed and sweating profusely. Not sure they had made the right decision; she searched Mark's face for signs of hesitation. *"Is that what you want to do?"*

"No. I want to get on that plane. But I want to know that you are right there with me. One way or the other, this is going to be an adventure. I just want to make sure you're ready to do this with me." His gaze never left her face.

"As ready as I'll ever be." Grace heaved a sigh of relief and relaxed. She held Mark tightly and closed her eyes. Worry gave way to expectation. *"God is in control. We can do this."*

CHAPTER XI

A Forever Family
Through The Eyes of a Child

Hepatitis A raged throughout the sanitarium. Procedural visits, allowing David to get comfortable with Mark and Grace over time weren't permitted due to the state imposed quarantine. This luxury lost, Tsemble brought David to Mark and Grace at the hotel.

David wasn't sure he liked this. It didn't feel right. He had a headache. He ached all over. Nothing felt right. A severe case of Hepatitis A clouded his thinking. Mark and Grace took custody of the same sad stoic little boy Grace had seen in the vision.

Later that week an adoption ceremony was held at the sanitarium. David wore a blue deel, the traditional, Mongolian silk robe. A gift from the sanitarium, it was his to keep.

According to Mongolian tradition a child is never given up. A child can, however, be raised by other family members. Lacking family members, another family can raise the child, but the child is not given to this family. This family is adopted into the child's family and then allowed to raise it. Once agreed upon, a bowl of mare's milk is passed around for everyone to share. Thus the transition is sealed. Mark and Grace were not adopting a child from Mongolia. Mongolia adopted Mark and Grace and allowed them to raise a Mongolian child.

"What a beautiful concept." Grace looked around the room at the smiling faces. *"Mongolians love their children."*

"How wonderful! What an honor." Mark's thoughts echoed Grace's.

They didn't understand much of what was being said during the ceremony, but they understood the smiling faces. Tsemble translated for them as someone handed David the bowl of mare's milk. *"You and Mark and David will drink out of this bowl and the covenant will be sealed."*

Panic reached down and took control. Laboring to breathe, a deepening tint of red color climbed Grace's neck onto her face. The beautiful ceremony had reached an impasse. Not drinking the milk would be rude, but Grace had no intentions of drinking after anyone with live active cases of Hep A, Hep B and Hep C. She hesitated. Everyone smiled and waited politely. Grace smiled back, her smile frozen on her face. She loved this child. She would protect and take care of this child for the rest of her life. Purposely exposing herself to deadly diseases however, didn't seem like a good idea.

Grace looked around. *"I may just have to do this."* Silently, she screamed out to her God. *"Lord, help me!"*

Mark's thoughts ran parallel to Grace's. *"What are we going to do? We can't insult these people. What are we going to do?"*

Reacting quickly to their hesitation, Tsemble reached for the bowl. She passed it to Grace before David had a chance to drink from it. *"You and Mark can drink first if you'd like,"* she smiled. Quiet sighs of relief escaped both Mark and Grace. Genuine smiles returned to their faces. The ceremony continued on.

Grace drank. Then Mark drank. Then David drank. Grace and Mark were now adopted Mongolians.

David had his forever family.

....

While David had heard about getting a forever family, he wasn't sure what it meant. He'd never experienced family life. They had explained it all before taking him to the hotel. Too sick to listen, he hadn't understood. Alone at the hotel he wondered if he had been taken away because he was sick.

A mere three years old, David had no clue what was happening. Sick and scared, lonely and confused, he clung to hope. He hoped this was his forever family and not the dreaded Children's Home. His only memories were filled with children and nannies. The nannies fed them and dressed them. They told them when to take a nap and when to use the potty. This was much different.

His first two weeks away from the Infant Sanitorium were spent alone with 'Aichy' and 'Owa' in the hotel in

Mongolia. They gave him a bath. That had terrified him, but he'd managed to fight his way out of the tub. They took him for long walks. They held his hands. They let him stay up late at night. They fed him wonderful food called ice cream. A forever family seemed like it could be a good thing.

When they got to Pennsylvania, David recognized his mistake. This was not a forever family. This was the dreaded Children's Home. It was larger than the room he lived in at the sanitarium, but not much different. Mark and Grace were no longer his Aichy and Owa. They were Mom and Dad now. David had solved this puzzle in his mind. *"That must be what they call their nannies."*

This Children's Home had eight other children. He was the youngest, as would be expected. The Children's Home was for older children. He knew that from what he'd heard at the sanitarium. This was lucky though. Since no one else wore his size, he didn't have to share his clothes anymore. Like the other nannies, the new ones fed him, washed his clothes and helped him dress each morning. Nothing had changed after all.

These nannies were pretty nice. They had given him a Mongolian, camel hair vest the first day they met. That was when he thought they were his Aichy and Owa. He wore it for three straight days, refusing to take it off. Mom and Dad - the new nannies – had let him sleep in it those first few days. They did wrestle it off of him though, to give him that bath.

Panicked at the thought of losing the vest, David had kicked and screamed. Doubt saw its chance and pierced his emotions. *"They won't want you. They won't want you. You're a bad boy. You're a bad boy."* Fear rushed in. It settled in his chest. Confusion followed close behind.

Fear, panic, doubt and confusion together terrorized David. Overcome, David sunk into silence. He was afraid to do anything else wrong. When the water torture was finished he found the vest waiting for him where he had taken it off. It had been a close call.

Here, at the new home, David learned he could wear the vest any time he wanted. No one else got a turn. It was his. Ownership was the first new concept David allowed himself.

Here there was no Aichy or Owa. How could he have been so confused? He had tried to call Mom 'Aichy', but again and again she corrected him. 'Owa' had become 'Dad' now too. Tsemble had promised him an Aichy and an Owa. She had been fooled by these people.

"Now I will never have a forever family." David wondered what had gone wrong.

On the airplane ride home he had been allowed to call them Aichy and Owa. He'd even found a picture in a magazine that looked just like Aichy. Shaking Owa till he woke, David showed him the picture. *"Owa! Owa! Owa!"* He pointed to the picture of a beautiful young woman with long blond hair. *"Aichy! Aichy!"* Proud of spotting his new Aichy in the magazine, David glowed.

Owa had woken Aichy to show her the picture. Aichy had laughed and hugged David. She had been so pleased with him. He felt proud. He felt loved. It felt good. Years later she would recall that moment. *"The model in that picture was half my age and half my weight. The moment I realized that that was how David saw me, I knew he was my forever child."*

When David so proudly mistook the picture of a beautiful young model for Grace, it had warmed Mark's heart. When Mark showed it to Grace a river of emotion flooded her soul. Love and joy overflowed their banks. They washed over David as Aichy laughed and hugged him. A bond was formed then and there between Mark and Grace and David that would never break. God had supplied a bond of love which no adoption proceeding could produce.

David understood none of this. He knew he loved these people he once thought of as his Aichy and Owa. He wished they loved him. He wished they were his Aichy and his Owa. They weren't, he knew, but he could wish. They were Mom and Dad. They had many children to take care of. He was just one of them. He would be obedient like the nannies had taught him. He wouldn't fuss. Then maybe they would love him too.

Often other nannies came to visit. They brought with them the children under their care. He played with these children for hours while the nannies talked.

These children all called their nannies 'Mom'. David, ever busy learning, called every nanny he met 'Mom' as well.

Grace wasn't amused by this. *"He thinks I'm his new nanny. He has no concept of parents or family."* It hurt a little.

"He'll figure it out. Give him time." Mark had much more patience than Grace.

"He thinks you're a nanny too. Or perhaps the maintenance man; maybe the delivery man." Grace made her point.

Grace did love the fact that David had been so well trained by the nannies. Whenever they came inside and took off their shoes, David would quickly line them up by the door. He lined up everything he saw. Toys, chairs, boxes, bars of soap. He threw everything else in the trash. If anyone left anything lying around the house for more than a few minutes, David dutifully threw it away. No one could find anything any more, but they all knew where to look. The house was never more well-kept.

"These nannies should open a summer camp for American children." Grace shot a glance towards her older children. She giggled when she told this story. She told it far too often for their comfort. *"Then they would all come home trained to clean up after themselves."* Her children were never quite as amused by this as Grace.

David remained prim and proper and polite. He didn't know what else to do. As stoic in Pennsylvania as he had been in Mongolia, he struggled to make sense of his situation. At the Infant Sanitarium, David had been the oldest. There he ruled. Here everyone else ruled over him. The nannies were right – this wasn't so nice. He began to notice a few more things.

Here they called him *'David'*. That worried him. They didn't know who he was. They hadn't realized their mistake yet. Maybe if they noticed he was the wrong boy, they'd send him away. He decided it was best to answer to *'David'*. Then he could stay.

They forced him to get into the water every day. They scrubbed him all over. He decided to accept this as well. It didn't hurt. It had scared him at first, but each time it got easier not to cry. In the end he gave up. He relaxed and let them wash him. After that he could play in the water for a while. Fear had lost its grip over bath time.

The food wasn't the same. That was for sure. They had tricked him with the ice cream. They almost never ate it here. Quietly, obediently he ate everything they gave him. The nannies had warned him not to waste food. David wanted these people to like him. He did everything the nannies had told him to do.

Sleeping alone was the worst. With rows and rows of cribs in one large room, David had never lacked company. He had never been left alone in the dark. Here he shared a room with Honorah, but she went to bed later than he did. Crying wasn't allowed. The nannies had taught him that. Lying alone in the dark, David fought the tears. Each and every night he lost the battle. Fear wrapped itself around him and overcame his ever loosening grip on control. Every night the silent tears flowed.

Recognizing the terror in her young son's heart, Mom capitulated. *"There's no reason to put him through this."*

"Admit it. He's your favorite."

"I love you all."

"Then how come we weren't allowed to stay up late?"

"It didn't terrorize you. You had each other. I can send you all to bed early if you'd like. Or he can stay up late. It's your choice."

No one ever won against Mom.

....

Unlike David, Honorah did like to sleep alone. Unhappy with her new roommate, she left David comfortless. When David tried to crawl into her bed she pushed him out. She mumbled words he couldn't understand. Scared he would pee in her bed, she wanted no parts of this intruder.

Night after night, Mom rocked David to sleep. After resting gently in Mom's arms, David would wake to find himself alone in his big, empty bed in the dark. Honorah, he knew, offered no consolation. Creeping down the long, dark hallway David would curl up on the floor of Mom's room till she woke. Sometimes Mom sensed his presence and took him into her bed. This was nice. He liked to be near someone when he slept. He liked to be near Mom. Sometimes Dad woke up first. Dad always put him back in his own bed. *"You spoil David,"* he told Mom. Dad never understood a fear of the dark.

The people from this home were always going someplace. The fear of being taken away rebounded each time they left the house. Scared and nervous, he threw up in the car - every time.

Often they went to a big children's home called 'church'. Lots of children his age lived there. This worried him the most. Pressed up against the door of the three year old room David waited quietly. Fear was his constant companion. It dogged his every thought. *"Why did they leave me? Will they come back? Did I line the shoes up well enough? Maybe this time they won't come back. I can't cry. They won't want me."*

Each time they rethought their decision to leave him there. They came back and got him. Seeing Mom again did little to assuage his fear or his confusion. He clung ever more tightly for fear she'd change her mind yet again. Arms wrapped around her neck, fingers grasping clumps of hair, head pressed against her shoulder, hidden tears of relief would have their way.

They also went to a place called 'the doctor's office'. This was a horrible place. They jabbed him with needles and sucked his blood. He knew if he cried Mom and Dad wouldn't want him. They would leave him there. So he never cried. He was a good boy.

Grace noticed everything about David. *"He never*

cries. He must be so scared." Her heart broke for her son.

One day they drove to a big white building called 'the hospital'. A lady with white clothes and a mask dressed him in a white robe. She put him on a cold bed and wheeled him away from Mom. His eyes never left her as they wheeled him down the hall. Other people strapped him down so he couldn't move. They shoved him into a big machine. Loud noise pounded his small body. Through all this David never said a word. He knew if he fussed, he would never see Mom again. Tears rolled down his cheeks. He couldn't stop them. Maybe they wouldn't notice.

They didn't. They never noticed. They brought him back to Mom. She had waited. He was sure that this time she would be gone. But she was still here. Being a good boy was so hard.

Mom always took the time to pick David up and hold him. She rocked him and sang to him. She tickled him to make him smile. Sometimes she cried when he didn't. She knew why he didn't cry. She knew he was scared. David liked this nanny. He hoped he wouldn't have to move again. He didn't want an 'Aichy' or an 'Owa' anymore. He liked this 'Mom' and 'Dad'.

Sometimes Mom would take them to 'the store'. Everyone loved to go to 'the store'. There were so many things to see there. Sometimes she would buy new clothes. Sometimes she would buy treats. Going to the store with Mom was more fun than going to 'the doctor'. She never took the other children to 'the doctor'. He was the only one still being tested to see if he would cry.

When Dad took him out he usually bought 'ice cream'. Mom told Dad that he needed to take him to 'the doctor' too. She was tired of being 'the meanie'.

After a while David didn't mind being called David. He became David. He was David. He noticed that Dad came home every night. He slept in the same house with them. He lived there. Maybe he wasn't the delivery man. He noticed that every time Mom went out, she came back. She wasn't going to leave them. He realized that whenever they left him somewhere, they always came back. He could play with the other children. Fear no longer ruled his days and nights.

Food started to taste better. David learned he could shake his head if he didn't like something. They knew what that meant. He could say *"No"*. That didn't always work, but David was learning that he could express himself.

Bath time meant that he'd be rocked and cuddled because he smelled so good. He preferred Sarah to do that. She had more time than Mom. She would cuddle him forever. He liked that.

David even noticed that Mom did a lot of special things for him that he'd never done before. She let him lick the spoon when she made a cake. She pushed him on the tricycle. She made sandcastles in the sand box. She read stories and taught him new words. Yet he never realized that most of all, Mom waited for him. She waited for David to understand.

The first year rolled by ever so swiftly. David became comfortable in his new home. His grasp of this new language had grown. The time had finally arrived for

Grace's much anticipated 'talk' with David. *"'Moms' only have their own children,"* she explained. *"You are mine. I am the only one you can call 'Mom'. There is no one else."*

"The dark haired 'mom' is Amelia's mom. The curly haired 'mom' is Faith's mom. The 'mom' with the big laugh is Bianca's mom. The tall, thin 'mom' is Margie's mom. The 'mom' with the short blond hair is Colleen's mom. I am your 'Mom'."

Mom meant Aichy.

Dad meant Owa.

David meant Gana.

David had his own mom. He was the right David. He had a real Aichy and a real Owa. There was no mistake. At last David understood. This was his forever family.

David was finally home.

CHAPTER XII

Learning to Lean on God

Having spent much time in prayer, Mark and Grace expected to see God's healing hand move in David's life. They weren't disappointed.

At the doctor's office David was tested and tested and retested again. The syphilis had been treated successfully in Mongolia with penicillin. Mark and Grace prayed that the long term effects be rendered null.

The Bible teaches that the sins of the fathers rest on their children. Thus, Mark and Grace reasoned with the Lord when they prayed. *"David is not part of that sin. He is innocent. He is a blood bought child of God. Forgive that sin please Lord, and make him strong and healthy. Give him a full, productive life."*

The Bible also teaches that whatever is bound, not allowed, here on earth will be bound in heaven and what is loosed, allowed, here on earth will be loosed in heaven. Jesus tells us that whatever we ask, we should ask *'in the name of Jesus'* and it will be done for us. So Grace and Mark bound sickness and loosed ministering angels of health. They prayed in Jesus' name.

"We bind up all sickness in David in Jesus' name and give it to Jesus. He paid for it. So we give it to Him to do whatever He wants with it. And Papa, we ask you to loose ministering angels of healing over David in Jesus' name."

They loosed the plans God had for David. They asked that He set His plans in motion. They prayed for wisdom for themselves and for David's doctors.

There is no formula for prayer. There is only faith in God. Grace knew that God has the power to heal. She believed that God had a plan for David, that He has a plan for all of us. From reading God's Word and hearing it spoken, faith comes to us all. The deeper our immersion in the Word of God, the stronger our faith grows. As faith grows, prayer becomes instinctual, just as it had with Grace.

Mark and Grace gave David large doses of Vitamin D to fight the rickets. Softened bones had already rounded his ribcage and bowed his legs. Because of this, his height remained steadily below the 5 percent mark on the growth chart, dipping perilously off the chart from time to time. Mark and Grace accepted the fact that David would always be short in stature. The truth, that God can change things, did not occur to them till much later. When the light of God's truth finally pierced the darkness of this dismal fact, they broke their agreement with this lie and watched as David grew into normal adult height.

As he grew, the doctor informed them that David was outgrowing the curvature of the spine. Another victory! Mark and Grace danced in praise. Their faith grew with each new triumph. God was allowing them an up close and personal witness to His love and His glory.

No new seizures occurred. For that Mark and Grace were truly grateful. Grace had quietly confided in God. *"It would be scary to watch my baby have a seizure. I don't think I could handle that. Please stop the seizures."* God knew what Grace could handle. There were no more seizures.

David had a fine, handsomely shaped head. It was not at all misshapen. However, it was huge. His head made up one third of his height. *"It still doesn't look hydrocephalic to me!"* Grace stood her ground. *"David does not have hydrocephalous!"*

She was right.

Grace knew, that she knew, that she knew, that David was not hydrocephalic. God had spoken to her about it in the vision. He had told her that David's head was *'just big'*. God had taken the time to point that out. It was truth. In this certainty, Mark and Grace never prayed about the hydrocephalous. They knew it was dealt with. They thanked God in advance for a good report and took David to the hospital to await confirmation.

David had been so brave that day. He had been strapped to a cold, white gurney and made to lie still in a shiny, white death-tube. The pounding machine palpated his terrified heart. Only a month into his life with Grace and Mark, he hadn't known what was happening to him. He didn't know where he was going or why he was there. He didn't know if Grace would be waiting when he got back. He didn't know if he'd done something wrong. He only knew not to cry.

Grace hadn't been allowed to accompany David to the CAT-Scan. Watching as David was wheeled down the hall, Grace was the one who cried. She knew the terror David felt. Waiting there that day, Grace cried all the tears that David had yet to shed.

Fully expecting a clean bill of health, Grace was shocked at the results. The report confirmed stroke damage from two separate strokes. *"How can you tell?"* Grace was incredulous. The tenor of her voice raised several octaves. The crying hadn't helped her composure, *"How can you tell how many?"*

"The CAT-Scan is clear." The doctor was as cold as the gurney on which they'd placed David.

This was devastating news. *"Damage to the brain – clearly seen – in two places?"* A sickening panic choked Grace's throat. Her head began to spin.

"There are no obvious side effects." The doctor looked at his chart. His voice droned on. *There is no hydrocephalous. His head is just big."*

The spinning stopped.

"Wait... I was right. God was right......Well, of course. God is always right.... It's good. It's really good. No hydrocephalous. No more seizures. No more strokes. No noticeable side effects from the

strokes. Not many people are this lucky." Grace looked around. She realized she was babbling.

Wondering what she must look like, Grace stood there, red-faced and blubbery from crying. Streaks of mascara smeared themselves across her wet cheeks. Quiet sobbing had turned to a high pitched panic at news of the strokes. Panic had emanated from her in the form of babbling. Emotion ruled over Grace like waves on the ocean, first rolling then breaking, one upon the other. No wonder the doctor had remained monotone. Lowering her head, Grace focused on the floor.

Regaining her composure, Grace picked her head up and politely thanked everyone. Bending over, she scooped David up, turned, and left the hospital. Behind her Grace left what remained of her shredded emotions. There, panic and doubt, ground into submission, watched as she walked out the door. Compassion she chose to keep. God was clearly in control. There would be no more roller coaster emotions.

Every day Grace looked at David's frail body and at his big head. She wondered how he managed to function. As an infant he hadn't lifted his head. Even now, at the age of four he couldn't sit up from a lying position. He rolled to one side and pushed up with his hands.

"I don't know how that tiny little neck holds up that big head. I would get tired of holding up something that big," Mark gave voice to Grace's musing.

When David stood, he used the strength in his legs to keep himself balanced. Sitting changed that dynamic. David didn't have the strength in his back to lift his head. Leaning in any direction was a proven recipe for disaster.

One time, without thinking, Mark set David on the hood of his car as he stooped to tie his shoe. David leaned over to see what Daddy was doing. He couldn't sit back up. Further and further the weight of his head propelled him forward. Mark glanced up just as David fell off the car, landing head first on the pavement. God in his wisdom knew David's head needed to be hard, so that is how He made it. Though tears were shed and a bump appeared, David remained largely unhurt. Undone by the sight he had witnessed, Mark never set David on anything above ground level again. It took time however, for a small curious boy to learn not to lean over.

....

Sarah adored David. She loved to play with him. What Sarah did, David did. She would clap her hands over her head then watch with delight as David attempted to imitate her. Up his hands would go, stretching to reach over his head. They never did. His arms were too short, his head too big to accomplish this particular task. Sarah laughed every time. She'd swoop down on David and gather him up. Covering him with hugs and kisses till both dissolved into laughter, they'd roll together on the floor in comedic embrace. Grace had to admit that humor was better than brooding over the size of David's head.

"One of these days he'll do it. You'll see." Grace rolled her eyes at them. *"That boy is gonna grow into that head."*

Eventually he did.

....

Syphilis, rickets, curvature of the spine, seizures, strokes and hydrocephalous had all been faced. Six down. Of the eight diagnoses, only two remained – Hep B and Hep C. On their first visit to the doctor Grace had received the paperwork necessary for the blood work. Eager to know whether David had Hepatitis B, or Hepatitis C, she followed through quickly. The answer to this question would frame their future.

The nurse poked and prodded to find a vein in David's four year old arm. He didn't cry when she drew his blood. *"What an excellent patient!"* she proclaimed. She never knew his pain lay deeper than the needle dare go.

Grace prayed hard as the blood was drawn. She understood Hepatitis B. Another son, born in Korea, had been a Hepatitis B carrier. She and Mark had watched and prayed over him for years. They had seen the Lord heal him completely. Grace knew what God was capable of.

Intimately acquainted with the statistics on Hepatitis B carriers, Grace knew they weren't good. Thirty percent of Hepatitis B carriers don't live past their teens. Another thirty percent don't get past 40.

Another thirty percent don't make sixty. Eight percent of Hepatitis B carriers do go on to live a normal life and die of normal causes. Two percent eventually develop antibodies and are no longer 'carriers'.

Anyone who contracts Hepatitis B will get very sick. It's not a good thing, but their bodies will produce antibodies. They go on to live a normal life. It's only when a child is exposed to Hep B at birth that they become carriers. An infant's delicate immune system is not developed enough to produce antibodies. Unable to fight the disease, the infant's body recognizes the disease as normal. This deception of normalcy continues to mislead the immune system. It never develops antibodies. It never fights the disease. The rest of their life, they carry a live, active case of this imposturous disease. Hence the term 'carrier'. Unhampered, Hep B ravages a carrier's body every day for the rest of his life.

This had been the case with Mark and Grace's older son. He was a carrier. Unlike the two percent of carriers who are eventually healed, Damon never produced antibodies. The virus simply disappeared. A prayer of faith offered on a missionary training base in Hawaii when he was 18, was the end of Hep B in Damon. Years of well documented test results are all that remain to prove he had been a Hep B carrier.

It was his miracle.

Grace was not unfamiliar with miracles. She'd seen God cure Damon. That's why she felt they could handle Hep B. They'd been through it once already. This thought had guided her prayers.

"Lord, we can handle the Hep B. We don't know anything About Hep C. We just don't think we can handle Hep C or a co-infection. We know Hep B is bad. We know Hep C is bad. A co-infection is a death sentence. Please don't let this be a co-infection."

"And Lord, you've put it into my mind that the Hep C could be a misdiagnosis. Lord let that be true. Let it be a misdiagnosis."

"And Lord, give us the faith and the strength to handle whatever he has. But we can handle the Hep B so much better than the Hep C."

Grace prayed her feelings, not the truth. She believed that Hep C was a misdiagnosis. She had discerned from the beginning that Hep B would be the only problem they would need to handle. So she prayed for the ability to handle Hep B. Grace prayed hard, but Grace prayed wrong.

There are two types of Hep B analysis. One test shows whether or not there are antibodies. This is the qualitative test. This shows that you have had Hep B and have developed antibodies. It doesn't diagnose a carrier. A carrier is a carrier because they have never developed antibodies.

The other test is called the quantitative test. It tells you the amount of virus per milliliter of blood. This is a much more difficult test to perform and takes much longer to obtain results. This is the test that must be run to diagnose a carrier.

The pediatrician called with good news. *"The results are negative. David has neither Hep B nor Hep C."*

"What wonderful news!!" Grace couldn't contain herself. *"Are you sure?"*

"Yes, the test shows no antibodies."

"Wait..... Isn't that the definition of a Hep B carrier? No antibodies. Which test did you run?"

"The qualitative."

"It's the wrong test." Grace wanted to scream. *"It's the wrong test!"*

"No, it's the right test. It's negative."

"It's the wrong test." Grace held her ground. She knew which test needed to be run.

The doctor finally agreed to retest. *"But he doesn't have Hep C,"* the doctor insisted. *"That was the right test."*

Uncertain, Grace continued to hold her ground. *"We'll retest for both."*

The retest showed the same results. Grace was livid. *"We know he doesn't have antibodies. They are telling us what we already know. We want the quantitative test."*

"The good news is that there is only one test for Hep C." The doctor remained calm. *"It's negative. We're sure of that. We don't need to retest that."*

Seven down. Another victory of faith had been scored. Either the Hep C had been misdiagnosed or

God had miraculously healed David. It didn't matter to Grace. No Hep C was all that mattered. No co-infection. Praise God. Only one disease remained left to fight. The sooner they found out what they were up against, the better.

Months and months of testing and retesting drug on. Each clinic ran the wrong test. The hospital ran the wrong test. Eventually the tests confirmed that David had Hep B but didn't show his viral load – the amount of virus in his system. These were the numbers Grace needed. Six months after beginning to test, Grace finally found a lab that would run the proper test.

The results were clear. Grace and Mark had gotten what they had prayed for. There was no Hepatitis C. A ferocious case of Hepatitis B, however, raged war on David's frail body. The Bible tells us that God will not give us any more than we can handle. Mark and Grace had repeatedly told God that Hepatitis B was something they could handle. Now they would be put to the test. They would spend years on their knees praying for wisdom and guidance, for strength and for healing for their young son. They would watch as David grew and praise God for every milestone passed. They would thank God every time his numbers went down and pray harder when things got worse. They learned to accept 'no' as an answer. Their patience grew. Their understanding grew. Their faith grew. Yes, they got what they had asked for. They also got so much more.

It took years before Grace realized this. She was sure that David's healing would come. She knew that God would use David's healing for a purpose. Grace wondered, however, if things might have been different if they had only prayed differently.

"Why do we try to handle things ourselves when we have such an awesome God?" Grace shook her head at her own foolish prayers. *"Why was I so insistent that we could handle this?"*

Grace prays differently now. She doesn't accept things into her life that are not from God, not even if she thinks she can handle it. Grace turns everything over to God. He is the God of healing, the God of peace, the God of Love, the God who is in control of all things. He is the God who loves us and has a good plan for us. When Grace embraced this truth, things got a little easier for her.

If we choose to hold to this truth, things can become a little easier for each of us.

CHAPTER XIII

Chemotherapy

The confirmation of David's Hep B was not a surprise. Mark and Grace had expected it. Though it often seemed like more than they could handle, Mark and Grace did know what to do. They knew the awful statistics. They knew what tests needed to be run. They knew the risk to family and friends. They knew that God was in control.

Hepatitis B is very similar to AIDS. It is a blood borne disease. It is sexually transmitted. It is also transmitted from mother to child at birth. It can be transmitted with the use of needles, or the exchange of bodily fluid. Changing the diaper of an infant of a Hep B carrier may relay the disease. Cleaning up after a bloody nose or an open wound with hands chapped from winter cold could result in the transfer of Hep B. Precautions need to be taken.

Mark and Grace and the entire family had been vaccinated after Damon had entered their home. Special care was taken with every bloody nose, lost tooth or open wound. The children were never allowed to share food or drinks – with each other or with friends. Close friends were informed of the circumstances. Only those vaccinated were allowed to attend to Damon or David's needs.

The Hepatitis B virus can live up to forty eight hours on any given surface. Runners have contracted Hepatitis B from being scratched by some bush along a jogging trail. Clorox in a spray bottle is considered the best solution for cleaning up Hep B body fluids. Grace kept a bottle handy for many years.

No one has ever been known to contract Hep B through any bodily fluids other than blood. If someone has, these cases are not well documented. Technically, however, it is still possible. Mark and Grace knew all this. After years of worry about contracting Hep B from Damon, Mark and Grace had become comfortable around it. Years and years of raising a carrier had not resulted in one single case of transmission among the Tinker family or friends.

This is why they felt they could handle Hep B. In this, they were correct. They didn't hesitate to wipe away tears to comfort either son. They never flinched when it came to pulling out a loose tooth, or wiping a snotty nose or administering first aid. They cleaned sheets that had been soiled by accident. They hugged and held and loved their children unconditionally – without fear. They handled this aspect of their children's health problems well.

The severity of David's case, however, was devastating. It took them off guard. It shook them to the depths of their faith. Damon's case had been a light one. The only thing they had done with Damon was monitor the virus regularly. With David regular monitoring wasn't enough. David's case required Mark and Grace to seek the counsel of a specialist.

CHOP - Children's Hospital of Philadelphia - and a pediatric gastroenterologist there, came well recommended by their pediatrician. It was a good hospital and it was close enough that they could go and return in one day. Mark and Grace decided that this would be the best place to seek treatment.

The doctor recommended chemotherapy. He hoped to bring the viral load down to a level where David's body could begin to fight the Hepatitis by itself. There were no guarantees. David's spiraling numbers convinced Mark and Grace to take action. They wanted to handle the Hep B aggressively. The sooner they were finished with this disease – the better.

The problem with chemo is that while it kills and destroys the virus it also kills and destroys everything else in the body. A patient is given chemo in the hopes that it does more harm to the virus than to the body. Then they hope that the body can recover. It's an awful way to treat a disease.

The worst part of the chemo was that Mark and Grace had to administer it to David themselves. Three times a week they had to inject David with this powerful killing medication. Three times a week they shoved a needle into his frail arm or leg or shoulder or stomach - any place that wasn't too damaged from repeated needle sticks - any place they could find that wasn't skin and bones on his emaciated body. The injection burned terribly. Three times a week they held him down as he thrashed and screamed. Three times a week they waited for David to get sick from the chemo. A day or two later, when David started feeling better, they injected him again.

At all times they were on guard against sickness. A common cold could have devastating effects on David's compromised immune system. Life became organized around the chemo; a cruel and heartbreaking life.

This was more than Mark and Grace were prepared for. Each injection grew worse. Each time the screaming grew louder. Grace cried every time she held David down. What was worse? Holding David down or injecting him with burning chemicals. Grace didn't know. She wondered if letting him die of this disease could be any worse than fighting it.

The first time they'd given David the shot he hadn't cried out. He'd gasped in surprise. He knew he wasn't supposed to cry. After the next time and the next time and the next time and the next time, David realized it wasn't going to stop. He gave up all pretense of bravery.

Grace would hold David still in her lap. Her arms wrapped around his arms. Her leg draped over his, to keep him still. Mark would come in quietly from behind. David wasn't fooled. He knew from the way 'Mom' held him that the needle was coming. He'd begin to thrash. 'Mom' held him tighter. The needle would stick. The burn would come, pain shooting in all directions. As the screaming gave way to a pitiful whimper Grace would loosen her grip. Now was her turn to cry. Unstoppable, the silent tears flowed. Gently she'd hold this frail gift from God, rocking him till he fell asleep.

Grace always cried along with David. David didn't know why, but it made him feel better. He didn't understand how, but he knew she felt his pain. Together they cried till the pain went away.

The first time was a bright, sunny day in late summer. Grace and Mark were warned that David might throw up for hours from the chemo. They were also warned that it might take time for the effects of the chemo to set in.

Grace was determined to be there for David when it happened. She laid a plastic tarp on the floor with some washable toys. After the shot they sat down on the floor together to play.

One hour passed and then another.

"David is handling this very well." Mark was relieved. *"I have free tickets to the baseball game. It's the last game of the season."*

"And it's the first day of your son's chemo. Take it seriously."

"I am. And he's fine. I wouldn't even bring this up if he were sick. But he's not. And I have these tickets. It's a waste not to use them."

"He could still get sick yet. They told us it could take a while."

"It's been a while. If he was going to get sick - he'd be sick by now."

Back and forth they argued till Grace conceded. *"OK, we can go to the game, but if he gets sick I will hate you forever."*

"*Deal,*" Mark yelled over his shoulder. He packed some drinks and snacks into the cooler. He called John and Peg and set up a meeting place at the stadium. Within minutes, they were off.

The ride to the stadium was blissfully uneventful. At the stadium, however, David threw up all over Mark. Unsympathetic, Grace glared at Mark. He had been warned.

In the restroom, Mark washed David and himself clean. David immediately threw up on Mark again. Cleaning David and himself up for a second time, Mark decided the worst was over.

Back at the stands, Mark handed David to Grace. John and Peg had joined her while Mark was in the restroom. *"He's past the worst of it now. No sense to leave now,"* Mark announced.

Grace kept control of herself. This was a public place. *"He's a little boy on chemo. He can't even hold his head up."*

John and Peg squirmed uncomfortably in their seats. They made no judgment calls.

"He'll be fine."

"He's not fine." Against her will, tears formed in Grace's eyes. *"Just look at him."*

David's eyes were shut. His head rolled to one side. He looked more fragile than she'd ever seen him look before. He was wet from vomit and from being washed up. A light wind blew down on them. David shivered with a chill. *"He's sick. We need to take him home."*

"There can't be much left in him to throw up. He's done."

"Then you hold him."

As Grace handed David back to Mark, David threw up yet again. Mark was covered in vomit for the third time. This was finally enough. They drove home in silence.

On the ride home David threw up again, this time on Grace. Though Mark scrubbed the inside of the van repeatedly, the odor refused to dissipate. For years it remained an unspoken reminder of the choices made that day.

Grace held David for the rest of that day. She rocked and comforted him. He had no idea what he was up against. Grace had no such luxury. She now knew what lay ahead. Although she never did hate Mark for what happened, Grace steeled herself against future possibilities. She needn't have worried. Mark never made a mistake like that again.

The side effects of the chemo, the throwing up and the listlessness, lessened after the first day. There were bigger and worse side effects to be had in the long run. David's attention span became shorter and shorter. After a year on chemo he could never sit still long enough to concentrate on anything. The doctors declared this a short term side effect. *"It won't last past the chemo."* They were overly optimistic. It did.

Another side effect of the chemo was asthma, severe asthma. David's immune system, compromised by the chemo had created a new enemy. Things were getting worse, not better.

For all their troubles, the chemo was ineffective. After an initial dip in his numbers, his viral load skyrocketed. It went from incredibly high to virtually uncountable. *"Lord, how much more can that little body take?"* Grace lifted David to God in prayer. *"What do we do now?"*

"Wait on me," God answered. *"Wait on me."*

So they did.

CHAPTER XIV

The Prayer of Others

David grew while Mark and Grace waited. He grew bigger and stronger and he came to know Jesus as his personal Savior. With the faith of a young child he told people about Jesus. This is how God calls us to believe - like a child – with complete faith. If you come to God without faith that He loves you, without faith that He sent His son to die for you, without faith that He has a plan for you or that He is in control, then you haven't come to Him at all. You haven't made Him Lord of your life. You haven't claimed Him as Savior. You haven't accepted all that He offers to each of us.

We can have questions. He wants us to ask questions. We can ask God to make Himself real. He will do that. We can ask for faith if we don't have it. He'll give it to us. We can ask for wisdom and understanding. God will give that to us too. The important thing is that we ask. The important thing is that we honor God by expecting an answer. Wait eagerly. The answer will come.

David had no questions. He simply knew that Jesus was real. He knew that Jesus died for him and that Jesus was his Savior. He knew that God answered prayer. That was all he needed to know.

His simple faith took Grace's breath away. She shook her head in wonder. *"What an awesome plan God must have for David's life. God has brought him through all of this for a purpose. What a wonderful testimony God had given David to share."*

Mark and Grace were constantly in awe of the power of God. The experts had told them David wouldn't live long. David was now thriving. The experts said he would be retarded and slow. David was bright and handsome and quick witted. David was a joy in so many ways.

"We could have left him there and no one would have blamed us." Mark recalled their conversation at the airport. *"But we'd never have seen the miracles God had planned for David."*

"And we'd have one less blessing in our lives." Grace stopped a moment to reflect. *"No, not one blessing, I've lost count of all the blessings."* She couldn't imagine life without David at this point. No one could.

If prayer healed David of many things it is because prayer was predominant in David's life. Mark and Grace read from the Bible and prayed with their children every day. They prayed over David every night before bed. They prayed more privately. They asked friends for prayer. They asked their church for prayer. They asked their extended family to pray. Very few people are ever the object of so much prayer. Then again, very few people face the challenges that David faced in his life.

It wasn't all growth and victories for David and Mark and Grace. Scars lined the landscape of their lives. At these times the whole community pulled together in prayer for David. People, who understand the power of prayer, often come before God for one another. Once someone grasps the idea that God answers prayer, it is only natural for them to pray for other people as well as for themselves.

The Bible tells us that the strong, insistent prayers of someone who is right with God, is very effective; the righteous, those who are right with God, those who have God in their lives, can pray and expect answers every time. This is the type of person you want praying for you in times of trouble or need. This is the type of person you need to be when you are praying for yourself or others. These were the kind of people who made a difference in Mark and Grace and David's lives.

The chemotherapy had been rough. Rougher still was the realization that it hadn't worked. David's numbers soared into the billions. Sometimes you can pray and pray. You do your best and it's still wrong. Hope fades. Depression takes over. Failure is all you can see. Past victories forgotten, it becomes harder to pray. Prayer becomes rote. It seems ineffective. It seems insignificant.

This is the pit into which Mark and Grace fell several months after David's fifth birthday. The year of chemotherapy had ended disastrously. Mark and Grace struggled through each day, trusting an unseen God for an unseen healing.

Early one morning David crawled into bed with them. *"My belly hurts,"* he whispered.

Bringing his knees to his chest, he repeated himself. *"My belly hurts."* His groanings filled the air.

Mark was cautious. *"What do you think?"*

Grace felt David's head. *"No fever."*

"Where does it hurt?"

"My belly."

Mark sighed. He was hoping to sleep in. *"Why don't you go lie down and see if you feel better."*

"It hurts." David didn't move. He lay on the bed, moaning.

"What do you think we should do?" Mark knew what Grace would say before he asked.

"Better not take any chances. He seems to be in pain. I can't believe he'd be faking. It's too early to get in to see the doctor. Better take him to the hospital."

Mark sighed again. It was five o'clock in the morning. The bed was warm and soft.

It was Mark's job to take the kids to the hospital in an emergency. Whenever Grace brought a child to the emergency room she waited and waited. If a child had a broken bone – she was treated like an abuser. If a child were sick - she was treated as if she were negligent. No such treatment was extended to Mark. The father of a sick or injured child was taken much more seriously than a mother. Grace had discovered long ago that her children received better care if Mark took them to the hospital.

Mark sighed yet again and got out of bed. *"Lay here with Mommy for a few minutes till Daddy can get ready to take you to the hospital."* David curled up tighter.

Grace held him close and whispered encouragement, *"Daddy will be ready in a minute. Just hang in there."* Silently she prayed. *"Lord, please give the doctors wisdom."*

Hours later Mark called from the hospital. *"David has a cold. He's having a hard time breathing. They've given him a shot. He should be fine. I called Dr. Chen on the way to the hospital and left a message. He just called back. He wants us to stop by his office so he can do a follow up. We'll be home after that."*

Grace breathed a sigh of relief. David had seemed so small and fragile that morning. She praised God for a good report and went gratefully on with her day.

The phone rang an hour later. It was Mark. *"You need to come to the hospital. David isn't doing well."*

When Grace arrived Mark filled her in on what had happened. In the parking lot near Dr. Chen's office David had collapsed. Too weak to go any further, he lay on the ground. Mark grabbed him and rushed into the doctor's office. Dr. Chen checked David's breathing. He called the hospital, furious, *"You released a child that has asthma so bad he can hardly breathe. I'm sending him back. Take him in immediately and put him in the asthma isolation room."*

Mark returned to the hospital. This time there was no waiting. David was taken directly to the pediatric asthma room. Half a dozen children in oxygen tents and on nebulizers filled the room.

This is how Grace found David when she got to the hospital. He was lying there listlessly on the cold white bed under a plastic oxygen tent. An IV dripped medication into his arm. Death hovered over David. A pale blue pallor enveloped his lifeless form. His lips were tinged an even deeper blue. Though his head rolled when Grace entered the room, David never acknowledged her. No smile came to his lips. No excitement danced in his eyes. No words came from his mouth. It was a hard thing to see.

He'll be OK in a few hours. We'll be out of here in six hours max. They want to monitor him for a while after his breathing comes back to normal. Then we can leave."

Grace looked at David and found no comfort from Mark's words. *"How is his stomach?"* She reeled at the sight of her son lying there so still. *"Is that Ok?"*

"There was nothing wrong with his stomach. He has asthma. It's so bad that he couldn't breathe. He was using his stomach muscles to try to push air into and out of his lungs. When that was finally too much he came to us, but he couldn't explain it. He didn't understand it himself. He just knew he couldn't do it any more. He could have died."

Looking death in the eye was more than Grace could bear. Every fear, every nightmare scenario she'd ever locked away rose up and swirled about her. *"What if we'd made him go back to bed? What if we'd waited to see if he felt better? What if he hadn't come in to our room? What if you hadn't called Dr. Chen? What if Dr. Chen hadn't told you to stop by? He'd be dead. He'd be dead right now."*

As much as Grace had steeled herself for the eventuality of this moment, standing there watching her lifeless son was all too real. They'd escaped death this time, but narrowly. Was it still lurking? Was it waiting for David? Had all of their best efforts come to naught?

Mark and Grace waited two hours; Then three; Then four.

"Twelve hours," they were told. *"He'll be fine in twelve hours. You'll be out of here soon."*

Twelve hours passed.

"Twenty four hours maximum," was the next promise given. *"You'll be out of here by tomorrow morning."* Grace spent the night. Mark went home to take care of the other children and to get some sleep.

Grace knew to call Grammy. She knew to call the church. At this point she and Mark needed prayer as much as David. Lack of sleep clouded their thinking. Fear numbed their minds. Too overwhelmed to think straight they sought the help of others.

When we are too tired to pray, when we struggle with unanswered prayer, when we have gone too long without a victory, when prayer seems rote and insignificant, we need help. The prayers of the righteous bring change. Mark and Grace knew this. They knew they were weak. They knew they needed strength. They knew they needed the prayers of the righteous.

The Bible tells us that if two or more of His people agree on earth concerning something, it will be done. The Bible tells us that if one can chase a thousand, then two can chase ten thousand. The prayer of agreement is a powerful weapon.

Grace knew this and she knew who the righteous were. The word went out. The righteous responded. Prayer washed over them there in the hospital. It continued for weeks. Too overpowered by their circumstances to pray effectively, Grace and Mark depended on others to stand in the gap.

One day turned into two. The battle for David's life shifted into high gear. Death bared its teeth and raged against prayer. The prayer warriors held their ground. Two days turned into three and three into four. Steadfast prayer continued. More warriors joined the crusade. Much needed ground was gained. Like a flood, prayer rushed in. The pallor left David's face. He opened his eyes. Four days turned into five and five into six. Unrelenting prayer weakened death's grip. David sat up and moved around. His lungs began to clear. On the seventh day David was released from the hospital.

His lungs still not clear, the battle continued at home. Hours were spent each day on the nebulizer. The cure for asthma, steroids in the nebulizer and the inhaler, compromised David's immune system even further than the chemo had. Uninhibited, David's viral load soared; Struggling now to fight both asthma and Hep B, David's only remaining line of defense was prayer. Death lingered, but the line held. Ever so slowly, David's health was restored.

Years were spent with an inhaler. The indoor environment needed to be controlled. Outdoor activity was restricted. Mark and Grace could have given up. David could have given up. But the prayers of the saints covered them. They were lifted with encouragement. They were empowered with the strength to go on. The battle for life was fiercely fought.

Prayer prevailed.

CHAPTER XV

Mongolia

In the summer of 2004, David turned five. Shortly after the asthma scare, Mark and Grace sold their business. A year later, in the fall of 2005 they moved to Hawaii with Moriah, Nick, Honorah and David. There they spent three months in a missionary training program and then, in the winter of 2006, they went on to China for the outreach phase of their training.

China was beautiful and exciting. It offered a strange, exotic blend of new and old, which charmed both Mark and Grace. A land of plenty, each street corner overflowed with different varieties of fresh fruits and vegetables to sort through and choose from. Aromatic smells emanated from sidewalk cafés. Old men played mahjong and young men set off firecrackers.

It was the perfect place for Mark and Grace to begin their work. Many people didn't understand the good news of the Gospel. They'd never been told they had a Savior. So many questions were asked and answers were so eagerly awaited. *"This would be a good place to serve God,"* Grace often thought. *"I like it here. There is so much need for the Word of God here. The people are so nice. If God were not calling us to Mongolia, I could serve God here."*

Mark concurred. *"I like it here too, but God gave us a vision for Mongolia."*

It was agreed. China had been added to their hearts. The place of their tent had been enlarged, but Mongolia remained the land of their calling.

With their training finished, Mark and Grace and their family went home and settled their affairs. They made arrangements to work for a university in Mongolia. By early spring in 2007, the Tinker family arrived in Ulaan Baator.

When you choose the God of Heaven to be your God, your heart longs to know Him more. In plain terms, you want to know what you are getting into, and what you are getting out of this relationship. When His promises and His blessings become real to you, your cup overflows, yet you want still more. You want all He has for you. You want to be where He wants you to be.

He may want you to be in school, learning all you can so you can serve him better. He may want you to be on the job, an example to all who see Him through you. He may want you to be at home raising Godly children or grandchildren. God has a different place and a different plan for each of us. We were not all made to do the same thing. However, a calling ignored is a life of missed blessings. God does not bless what we do not do.

If you are called to take a sick and dying child into your home and raise him as your own, and you don't do it, you might miss your blessing. Mark and Grace, never were ones to miss a blessing, had watched David grow stronger and healthier as the years passed. Their business had prospered. Relationships had flourished. Their faith, often tested, had grown secure. Now they were blessed to be in Mongolia. Life with the Lord remained an adventure.

Here in Mongolia, Grace and Mark served at the Jesus Love Church in Baroon Selah. They taught English at Mongolia International University. They held Bible studies in their home for the students. They shared God's word in several children's homes nearby. These young children with no earthly fathers to love them or care for them listened closely. One by one they chose Christ as Savior. Child by child, their Heavenly Father stepped forward to fill the father-shaped hole in their hearts.

At Christmastime, thousands of candy canes arrived from home. It was exciting to receive them in the mail. The candy canes opened a new avenue to share the story of Jesus.

These hard, white candies are shaped like a shepherd's cane which represents Jesus as our great shepherd. He watches over us. The white represents the purity of Jesus, the perfect sacrifice for our sins. The hardness represents the trials He suffered to save us from our sins. The sweetness represents the sweetness of God's love and His promises. The minty taste is refreshing. This represents us. Our spirit is made alive within us. We are born again. We are new creatures in Christ.

The red stripes represent the blood of Jesus. It represents His sacrificial death. It represents all the sins that are covered by his blood. It represents the healing power of His blood. The Bible says, *'by His stripes we are healed'*. These stripes are the stripes laid on His back by the whipping Jesus suffered for us so that we don't have to. Because He suffered for us, because he took our sickness and our diseases to the cross, we can be healed.

This is the good news of the cross. Not only do we receive salvation and blessings when we walk with Jesus, but He also takes away our sickness. He removes our guilt. We are washed clean.

The candy cane is a clear picture of Christ and of Christmas, the gift God had given us. The candy canes afforded Mark and Grace the opportunity to tell hundreds and hundreds of people about the love of God. Many accepted Jesus as Savior. Many more brought candy canes home to share the story of Jesus with their families. What a blessing to share a candy cane.

"I could spend my life telling these people about Jesus," Grace ruminated out loud over that thought. She loved seeing the light of Jesus shine through the eyes of new believers.

Mark's eyes danced with approval. *"Then let's stay here and do that."*

In agreement, the plan became set.

....

Our plans, however, are not always God's plans. Doing good things and asking God about his plans are two different things. Mark and Grace had yet to learn this lesson.

During their time in Mongolia, Mark, Grace and the children participated in a television series about foreigners in Mongolia. In the interview Mark and Grace discussed adopting David. They discussed God's hand in healing him. This segment was shown several times a week. People began to recognize them where ever they went. Mark and Grace giggled at their notoriety. *"I guess we do stand out in a crowd."*

The show's producer ran into Mark at the grocery store. He asked them to do a follow-up segment. *"People want to see how David is doing."*

"We get David's viral load checked every six months," Mark explained. *"When we have good news about his Hepatitis B, we'll come back and film another segment."*

"It's a deal!!"

They shook on it.

Mark informed Grace about his conversation with the producer. This sent her imagination rolling in high gear. Grace envisioned telling all of Mongolia what God had done for David. But while David's numbers often fluctuated - sometimes higher, sometimes lower - there was no healing to speak of.

"Oh Lord, it's such a good plan." Grace had grown tired of waiting for David's healing. She pressed her point. *"If you heal David we can go on television and tell the world. Why isn't this your plan? What's wrong with this plan?"*

It was a good plan. It was a wonderful plan. It, however, wasn't God's plan. His silence rang in Grace's ears.

Grace knew that when God says *'No,'* He often has a better plan. If you are praying for a spouse, the person you are hoping for might not be the person God has for you. His answer will be *'No!'* Rejoice in *'No'*. A much better *'Yes'* awaits. The Bible tells us that He will give us more than we could think or ask for. When God says *'No!'* we need to be patient.

Grace knew this. She had learned this lesson many times. When she and Mark were newlyweds, Grace had found a lovely home for their growing family. She begged Mark to make an offer on it. Instead, Mark had waited. Day after day drug by, seemingly without serious consideration of Grace's desire for a family home. Mark hesitated. Mark stalled. Mark balked. When he finally relented and placed a bid, an offer had been accepted forty-five minutes earlier. There was no house for Grace.

Self-pity knew when and where it was welcome. Grace had rolled out the welcome mat. Together they threw a party. No one else came because no one else was invited. No one else seemed necessary. Grace had found a new companion.

A month later, Mark did find a house in their price range. It was a beautiful house, a log cabin built by a Canadian logger. It was not only bigger, but it also came with more property and more privacy. It was perfect for them and their growing family. It was God's better plan for them. Self-pity took a hike that day, by himself.

God had a better plan for David also. Grace understood this, but she still liked to complain. She liked her plan. She wanted David healed as soon as possible.

As always God laughed at Grace's impatience. His patience with her matched her impatience with Him. She would learn, He knew. It never disturbed Him when Grace came to Him with questions and complaints. He loves his children to turn their attention on Him.

Grace watched as David grew. As he grew his body became stronger. Perhaps now, Grace hoped, his body would begin to produce the antibodies he needed to fight this unrelenting disease.

This wasn't to happen. Death again flared its nostrils. Death bared its fangs and growled a terse warning. This disease which had never shown David a days rest, never tired from attacking his liver, now threatened to bring an end to his young life. David's liver had begun to harden.

"The liver is the only organ in the body that can regenerate itself," Mark and Grace encouraged each other. *"There is always hope that things will change."*

David's numbers, the amount of virus in his body, rose and fell, but it was never comforting. Whether you have hundreds of millions or billions of pieces of virus per milliliter of blood in your system, it makes little difference. There is a point where the numbers cannot be accurately counted. David's viral load had reached these numbers. The doctors hoped that if the numbers fell below a million parts per milliliter, his body might take over and produce antibodies. But for now his numbers hung in the two billion range, too high to accurately count.

By the time David was seven years old his liver was seriously hardening. *"We'll have to begin to actively treat him again,"* the doctor told them. He ordered a liver biopsy.

"No more chemotherapy." Mark and Grace were united on this.

"It may be our only choice," the doctor replied. *"There is new research and new drugs coming on the market all the time. The longer we can wait the better, but we can't wait too long. Once the liver becomes too hard, it's too late. But for now, the biopsy shows that we have a year."*

They waited the year and the doctor gave them another. The next year, the summer that David turned nine, there were traces of antibodies in David's blood. A trace was not nearly enough to handle the billions and billions of viruses in his system. A trace of antibodies, however, was a trace of hope.

"Don't get too excited. It's only a trace." The doctor's tone conveyed warning, but he was talking to the wrong people. A trace of hope, mixed with a lot of faith is a powerful alloy. That was what He was doing for Mark and Grace, giving them hope to mix with their faith.

They traveled back to Mongolia later that summer with a song on their hearts. It promised to be a very good year indeed.

And it was, for a while.

Then the cold wind began to blow.

CHAPTER XVI

The Vision Unfolds

In the early summer of 2007, a vivid dream woke Grace with a start. It left her sweating, unable to breathe. In her dream she had woken up earlier. She had gone about her daily routine and ended up at the store shopping for groceries for dinner. There, at the store, she ran into the television producer. They discussed the show and doing a new segment, but Grace didn't take him too seriously. *"We don't have good numbers for him yet. There's nothing new to tell. And besides, it's too much to tell on a half hour segment."*

The producer agreed heartily. *"Then you must write a book all about David's life for the Mongolian people. When you do that, I will have you back on the television show to tell people about the book. Promise me you'll do that."*

"I promise," Grace agreed enthusiastically. *"I can do that."*

They shook hands and the deal was struck. A warm sensation of heat and light flowed through Grace's hand as she shook the producer's hand. It surged up her arm and into her body. The producer stood smiling at her. As Grace felt the warmth flow into her body from the producer's touch she realized that it was not the producer she was talking to. It was God.

It was God that told her she must write the book about David's life for the Mongolian people. It was God to whom she had given her promise. It was God who was arming her with the strength and the encouragement she needed to write this book.

"I'm talking to God. I promised I'd write a book." This realization stunned Grace. Waking up surprised her even more. It had seemed so real. It was hard to believe she'd been dreaming. Sweating and unable to breathe, she was filled with fear and trembling and awesome wonder. *"I talked to God,"* she thought. *"I promised God I'd write a book."*

For days Grace pondered this.

God often communicates with us through dreams. The Bible is full of stories in which God speaks to people in dreams. It still happens today. Dreams are similar to visions, except they're much more common. Many people have dreams from God and don't realize it.

Like visions, dreams often need to be interpreted. For the interpretation of a dream or vision we need to press closer to God. We need to ask Him for the interpretation. Then we need to listen for His answer. This is part of God's plan for us. He wants us to walk with Him and talk with Him, to ask Him questions and to listen for answers.

This dream needed little interpretation. The producer represented a man in charge, a man who wanted to present David's story to the Mongolian people. Grace represented herself in the dream. You are always yourself in a dream or vision. Sometimes you also represent your spouse or your family. In this dream Grace had an encounter with the producer, the man in charge, in the midst of her daily routine. In real life Mark and Grace were going about what they needed to do, teaching, holding Bible studies, preaching at the church, and Grace had an encounter with God.

In the dream the producer/God had told Grace that He was interested in doing a follow up on David for the Mongolian people. *"Imagine that!"* Grace reflected on her dream. *"God told me He was interested in David. He wants to tell the Mongolian people about David. And I told Him that David's numbers weren't good enough yet."*

While Grace and Mark were doing good things in Mongolia, God was now calling them in a different direction. In life, as in the dream, Grace realized that she had promised God she'd write the book. In life, as in the dream, she didn't take it too seriously.

Grace always knew she would write the book. She had promised God, after all. She was ecstatic that God had chosen her for such a job. She had every intention of writing it – just as soon as she had time, but first she had a university department to run. She'd finish up the exams and get started working on the book over summer break.

With only a few weeks off from school the summer was short. It slipped away before anyone noticed. There was always so much to accomplish on their short visit home. Grace rationalized, *"During the fall semester it will be easier to get started."*

Of course that didn't happen. The school year was full of students and staff and decisions and plans, meetings and needs and requirements to fulfill. *"This winter I'll start."* Grace was firm in her decision.

Over winter break Grace decided to get some course work towards her Pastoral credentials out of the way. She had finished thirty courses. She was a licensed pastor but ordination was within reach. *"Three more courses and I'll be done. Then I can start the book."* Two of the three courses were completed over winter break, but the book remained untouched.

"I'm running an English School. I'm preaching on the weekends. I'm having Bible studies during the week. I help home school my kids. How can I get to the book during the school year?" Grace was in a pickle. *"I'll do the last ordination course over summer break and work less next semester. Then I can start the book."*

The spring of 2008 came and went.

Summer break back in the States also came and went. The last ordination course was completed. Doctor visits, dental visits, home and car maintenance issues were all dealt with. At every turn, there were more things to tend to, than time to tend them. No time remained to start writing the book.

Any Christian knows that God expects obedience from His people. Obedience brings blessing. He loves us and cares for us. He is patient and kind with us. In return for all that He gives us, He expects us to be obedient to His calling. He calls us to obey His commandments. As children of God we are not to lie or cheat or steal or gossip or worship other gods. We are to honor our parents. We are not to be jealous of others. We do not kill others.

We are to honor our bodies because God's Holy Spirit comes on us and lives in us when we accept Jesus as Savior. The Bible tells us that we become one with Christ – just as He is one with God. We are to become like Him.

We are to obey God when He tells us to do something. If He whispers in our ear that we need to abstain from alcohol, then we need to abstain from alcohol. If He makes it clear that we are to be kind to a stranger, then we need to be kind to that stranger. If He tells us that we need to write a book, then we need to get started writing that book.

Slow obedience is no obedience and Grace's obedience was very slow indeed. Grace had every intention of writing the book, yet over a year had passed and the book remained untouched.

The fall semester began with fewer hours at school. Mark took over the Bible studies and the weekend preaching. Grace, however, found herself dedicated more and more to her children's education. She'd home school David till 1 in the afternoon, then teach at the university till five or six. She stayed at school and did paperwork while Moriah took Russian class. By the time they got home it would be seven o'clock at night. Grace was too tired to write.

The book began to weigh heavily on Grace. She knew what God had asked of her. She also knew she was not honoring God. More than anything in the world, she wanted to honor God, not because she feared God, but because she loved Him with all her heart. Grace wanted to be obedient. She knew that God was patient, but she also knew that she was moving further and further away from God's plan for them by this act of disobedience. It all seemed to be out of her control. She had planned and planned and tried and tried to get the book started, all to no avail. Time consistently eluded her.

God was patient. He knew Grace's heart. He knew she wanted to write the book. He also knew that in her busyness, it would never happen. There were too many demands on her life. She couldn't do it all. She would if she could, He knew that, but she just couldn't do it all.

Gently he began to whisper in her ear. *"Your season is done here. You need to go back home and write the book for me."*

"Oh Lord, how can we leave our students? I love this job. You gave us these jobs. How can we leave the church? How can we leave this country? You put us here."

"Your season here is finished," God pressed gently. *"You need to go home now."*

"I need confirmation, Lord." Grace had grown weary. She knew their season there was finished. She felt it deep within herself. She didn't know how they'd do it, but they needed to go home in the middle of their contract with MIU. They'd also signed a full year contract on their apartment. Grace knew Mark would need more than her word that God was telling them it was time to go home. Mark took a lot on faith when God spoke to Grace, but this would be too much. *"If you want us to go home, you'll have to talk to Mark too,"* Grace whispered back to God.

If God talked to Mark, then Mark wasn't listening. He had no plans to go home in the middle of the school year. He had no desire to make any plans either. He was adamant. *"We planned to stay here two more years after this year."*

"I know," was all Grace managed to say. *"That was our plan, but we never asked God what His plan was."*

"Well, it's a good plan. We've only been here for two years. There's nothing for us back home. We have no reason to go. Christmas is almost here. We've asked people to send candy canes again. I can't believe God would want us to leave without seeing that through. If God wants us to go home, He'll give us a sign. I need to have a sign."

So a sign is what they waited for.

While they waited God spoke gently to Grace. He reminded her of the vision she had had all those years ago. He opened it up for her. He showed her details she hadn't noticed before.

God reminded Grace that she had been sitting in the front of the wagon. She was driving the wagon. This, He told her was representative of her running the English School at the university. There, at the school, she was in the driver's seat.

He reminded her of how she felt about giving up the seat on the wagon. He reminded her how she felt about stepping down. She remembered how hard she had struggled making the decision to leave the wagon. She'd put it off again and again. In the vision she wanted to stay with the wagon, but she knew what she had to do. She knew what God expected of her. She had to step down and take care of the children he'd given her.

God reminded Grace of how much the baby girl in her vision resembled her daughter, Honorah. *"The baby in the vision was Honorah,"* God whispered in her ear. Stunned, Grace recalled that she had been unable to conceive naturally at that time. Premature ovarian failure, the doctors had called it. Grace had turned to fertility drugs. *"She is a gift of love that flowed from Me to fill the desire of your heart. David was also a desire of your heart from the day you saw him in the vision. These are the children I have given you."*

Honorah had come to Grace as a baby. David had come as a small child. That was why Honorah was a baby in the vision and David was a young child. In real life Honorah was four years older than David, but in the vision God gave them to Grace exactly as he had in real life.

It now made sense to Grace. The pieces were falling into place. She had always wondered why the baby in her vision was so blond, why the baby had looked so much like Honorah. Of course, it was Honorah.

God showed Grace that Mark, as her husband in the vision, had represented Jesus. God's word tells us that Jesus is the bridegroom. We, His people, are His bride. It was not Mark who gave Grace those children. It was Jesus. It was Jesus who was standing beside the wagon. It was Jesus who was gathering children in Mongolia for the Lord. It wasn't Mark and Grace gathering children for Holt International Children's Services as Grace had imagined. It was Mark and Grace, together on the wagon, helping Jesus to gather children for the Lord.

This also now made sense to Grace. She and Mark had always worked together. She could never understand why, in the vision, she had to make a choice to stay with Mark or to leave the wagon. She couldn't understand why she was teaching and he was gathering children, and why they needed to be apart.

In her vision Grace represented both Mark and herself. They were always together. They had never been apart. They didn't need to be apart. They both were teaching at the school together. They were running the Language department together. They were also both helping to pastor a church. They were together *'on the wagon helping Jesus to gather children for the Lord'*. They both loved what they did and they both struggled with the decision to leave the wagon.

Grace now understood why Mark needed a sign. He was struggling as much as she had with this decision, only he'd never seen the vision. To him the vision wasn't as real as it was to her. He couldn't replay it in his head. He needed a sign.

God reminded Grace of the cold wind that blew across the wagon, forcing her to make the decision. The cold wind meant that the season had changed, that they weren't prepared for the next season. They needed to get down off the wagon. Grace found peace with her newfound revelation. Yet still, she worried about Mark. *"Please, please, please give Mark a sign."*

In life as in the vision Grace acknowledged their season here was over. Yet, leaving burdened her heart. *"Who will take our place Lord? Who will preach at the church? Who will hold Bible studies for these kids?"*

"You are getting off the wagon," Jesus gently explained. *"I will stay with the wagon. Your season is over. Mine is not. I will stay in Mongolia and gather the children the Father calls Me to gather."*

Grace was overwhelmed by this new revelation. "Of course Jesus stays with the wagon," she thought. *"Of course, Jesus is always there for us. How comforting to know that the work will go on. How comforting for the people of Mongolia to know that Jesus will be with them no matter who comes and who goes. God is so good!"*

Grace continued to wait for Mark to realize that their season was over. Mark wasn't so easily convinced. Things were going well. The work of the Lord was being done. They'd recently decided to stay for at least two more years. He had no desire, no plan, to leave Mongolia and head back to the States.

He'd yet to feel the cold wind blow.

CHAPTER XVII

Growing in Favor with God and Man

Through all these years of chemo and missionary training, living in China and Mongolia, David grew and grew. He grew from a sad, serious child into a loud, boisterous child. Surrounded by family and friends, he grew in strength and health and in favor with God.

Favor with man arrived more slowly. David feared nothing. Without thinking, he would blurt out the wrong thing at the wrong time. Keeping his thoughts to himself was beyond his grasp. If he thought it, he said it. *"Think before you speak!"* his siblings groaned in exasperation.

"Lord, please help him to outgrow this," Grace constantly prayed. *"Please give him wisdom, understanding and self-discipline as well as self-confidence."*

"And Lord, please give all my children, all that you have for them. Give them gentleness and kindness and goodness and meekness, temperance and faith, love, joy and peace. And give them wisdom and understanding and compassion. Make them diligent and give them a desire to know you. Please prepare them for their future spouses and prepare their

future spouses for them. And Lord, please give them the desire to raise their children in You."

"Lord, fill them to overflowing that they might not only know you, but that they would tell others about you. Put people in their path and people in their lives that would sharpen them and challenge them and encourage them to know you better, and let them be sharpeners and challengers and encouragers to others."

"Let this house always be a house of prayer and a house of praise, a house of rest and of refuge. Lord you are always welcome here. Let your wisdom and compassion, let your mercy and grace dwell here always. Let this be a house of sweet dreams. Let this be a house of healing and a house of strength; A house of love. A house of refreshing."

"And Lord, please, watch over them while they are away from us and always bring them home safely to us. Convict them when they are in sin. Forgive them and show them that your ways are higher than their ways. Let them walk in blessing and let them always see your hand on their lives."

"Give them strength and health and self discipline. Give them dreams and visions. Put a song in their hearts. Let them love one another. Let them help each other and hold one another up before you."

"Lord let them have Godly friends. Let them find good relationships, where they can grow in You. Let their homes be filled with You. Bless them Lord, bless

them. And always let them know that it is from You that their blessing comes."

Yes, David, his siblings and their home were all washed in prayer. That didn't mean they were all perfect, or even that Grace was perfect. It meant that they were covered in prayer. It meant that God, who hears our prayers, especially the prayers of a praying mother, was watching over them. He was ready to forgive them when they made a mistake and ready to bless them when they put Him first.

Like everyone else, they still had the choice to choose God or to turn away from Him, to prefer sin and selfishness over forgiveness and blessing. Grace couldn't make them choose God. God is a gentleman. He doesn't ever make anyone choose Him. He waits patiently, always ready for a relationship with all who call on Him. As He waited for David's mother, He waits for Grace's children. He waits for all of us.

David, growing up in a Christian home, naturally grew in knowledge of the Lord. There was also, of course, much he didn't understand. One day he questioned Grace. *"Mommy, is God our God or is it Jesus? And who is the Holy Spirit?"*

"God is God," Grace explained. *"He sits on the throne in heaven. Jesus is a part of God. Jesus is God."*

"Jesus is a god?"

"No, Jesus and the Holy Spirit are both part of God."

"Three gods?"

"Three separate gods would be fighting with each other. So, no, just one God in three parts. Just like us. We have a body, a soul and a spirit. Our body is what people see. Our soul is the way we think and act, is also who we are. And, it is our spirit that communicates with God when we ask Jesus to be part of our lives. God loves us just as much as He loves Jesus, because He sees Jesus in us."

"Then we're perfect?"

"No," Grace sighed. *"We can still make wrong choices. And we do."*

"Are we brainwashed?"

"Nope. Not at all. We always get to choose. We have to choose. We can forgive and be a blessing or we can choose anger and hatred and greed and unforgiveness. It's hard to choose most of the time. But the more we get to know Jesus, the more we want to be like Him."

"I'd like to be like Jesus."

"You are," Grace assured him. *"You're my little blessing."*

It was in the late fall of 2008, as David's frail body grew stronger and stronger, that Grace's own health began to fail. Years of cramming every spare minute with work had taken its toll. Grace's blood pressure rose well beyond manageable levels. Her heart raced, even in a resting position. Panic attacks became routine.

The panic gave way to higher blood pressure and higher pulse rates. Higher blood pressure and an elevated pulse gave way to increasing panic attacks. Grace's body pulsated with every beat of her heart. Her chest tightened. Thoughts raced through her mind more quickly than she could grasp them. Though her heart and mind raced, her mouth refused to work. Forming words, thoughts, sentences became impossible. The world spun out of control. Grace felt as if she would literally explode. *"Lord, show Mark. Show him we need to go home."*

Grace besieged God in prayer at every opportunity.

Tired of waiting, she became insistent with Mark. *"We need to go. I can't do this any more. I am sick. I am exhausted. I am not getting any better. And God is telling me that we need to go."*

"Well, God hasn't told me anything yet."

"Fine. We'll wait." Grace clenched her already tightened jaw. She took tranquilizers to keep her heart rate down. She took the blood pressure medicine the doctor had given her in increased doses. She took herbal medications. This would have to do till God spoke to Mark. All the while her symptoms worsened.

By late fall Grace was severely short of breath. Walking from the car to her office disoriented her. If she closed her eyes the world spun. She'd lose her balance. Grace considered giving in to it. Falling down, might be the best thing. If people realized she wasn't well, she could quit trying to seem normal.

Functioning on the lowest level possible, Grace barely managed to hold on. She missed classes. Mark covered them. She missed church. Mark asked everyone to pray. She informed the school that she would not teach in the spring. The staff at school lifted her in prayer. *"If I die here, will it be a sign?"* she asked herself.

One day, on the way home in a cab, Grace shut her eyes for a second too long. She swayed unsteadily in her seat. Vertigo played with her, calling her into a sea of nothingness. Afraid of the consequences, she refused to let go. Her pulse began to race, faster and faster. Her blood pressure rose, closing her throat. Her neck burned. Her face burned. Her eyes rolled. The pressure cooker in her head found no release valve.

Grace hung on. She clutched the seat. She tried to breathe. Her chest tightened. Speech disappeared. Reasoning hung by a thread.

"We're here, Mom," Moriah announced.

Grace struggled to get out of the cab. The cold air hitting her face revived her long enough to make it up the stairs into the apartment. Reeling from the experience, she dropped onto the couch. A low buzzing sound, like that of a truck shifting gears, competed with an intense ringing in her ears for priority inside her head.

When the pain in her chest subsided, Grace looked Mark straight in the eyes. *"I don't know what more you need,"* she said, *"but I'm done. I almost had a heart attack in that cab. You're waiting for a sign? Is that good enough for you? Because it's good enough for me. I'm not going to die here in Mongolia waiting for you to get a sign. I'm going home to get treatment. You do what you have to do. I have to go home."*

Incredibly, Mark still argued the point. *"Do you expect us to go with you? Do you expect to come back? We have a contract with the school. We have a lease on the apartment. We can't afford to all go home. When will you be better?"*

"I can't afford not to go home." Grace was too sick to argue any further. All she knew was that she had to get home. *"And I can't predict when I'll be better. It might be a few weeks. It might be never. I can't tell you! But I am going home. You decide what you need to do."*

Mark realized how serious it must be for Grace to make this decision on her own. He'd hoped it would all blow over. He'd hoped Grace would feel better. But now, he realized, that wasn't going to happen.

Deeply disappointed, going home didn't feel right to Mark. Grace could go. He'd help her with that, but he was determined to stay until the Christmas season was over. He'd see the school through till the end of the semester. He'd see the church through till Christmas. Then he would come home.

Grace didn't care. She was too sick to care. She felt defeated. She had hoped God would give Mark confirmation that this was His plan. She'd hoped he'd receive a word, a dream, a vision, anything. In her mind Grace had pictured them walking side by side, holding hands, encouraging one another, standing firm in the Lord, following His every leading. In reality she was going home alone.

"I'll take David and Honi with me so you can work without having to take care of anyone. Moriah and Nick can stay and help you." Grace knew that the work was important. She knew Moriah and Nick wanted to stay. Although she wanted Mark home with her, Grace was happy he'd finish the work they had started together. She was also glad for some time alone. Going home to rest and to heal would be easier to do without the whole family there.

It was only when they were on the plane that Mark realized Honi and David were much too young to take care of Grace if she suffered a heart attack at home. They lived in the countryside, miles from stores or doctors. For this reason Mark sent Moriah home immediately after the semester ended. It was an emotional farewell. After saying goodbye to her friends, Moriah traveled home alone. She cried for days afterward. Mongolia had been indelibly written on her heart.

CHAPTER XVIII

The Plans I Have for You

It was mid November, 2008, when Grace, David and Honi arrived back home in the States. Uriah and Cheyenne were there to pick them up at the airport. Moriah arrived just before Christmas, on December 23rd. Malachi got to the house on December 24th. Mark and Nick flew in on December 29th. Sarah got in on the 1st of January, 2009. Having almost everyone together was a healing balm for Grace's heart. *"God is so good,"* she thought.

At home, an unseasonably cold November had greeted Grace and the kids. The heater was broken and repairs took a few days. In the meantime they used the wood stove for warmth. While this presented no problem, had they not come home when they did the pipes would have frozen and burst. Untold damage and tremendous expense would have resulted. Grace informed Mark of this when he called from Mongolia. *"It's a sign that we were meant to be here."* He had to acknowledge it was a good thing that they had come home when they did. *"God is good,"* Grace pointed out.

Shortly after he returned home, Mark's mother passed away. His father had passed away years before. The week before she passed away Mark and the kids had gone to visit her. They spent a pleasant afternoon together. She died unexpectedly the next week. *"God is so good,"* Grace repeated herself. *"If we hadn't come home, you might not have seen her before she passed away. God is taking care of us and letting us know that we need to be here. This is His plan."*

Mark only mumbled his acknowledgement.

"How many signs does he need?" Grace wondered.

Month after month Grace went back and forth to the doctor. One new medication after another was tried. Tremendous side effects accompanied each new trial. Each side effect seemed worse than the last.

"Let this be it, please Lord," Grace prayed. *"Let this be the cold wind that blew. Let it be my health. And let this season be over. Please don't let the cold wind be David's health. Please Lord. Let him develop real antibodies, not just a trace. Let his numbers come down. Give him his healing miracle. Please don't let bad numbers be Mark's sign that we need to be here."*

Grace feared this cold season. In the vision God had expected them to get down off the wagon to take care of the children He had given them. What special care might they need here in the States that they couldn't get in Mongolia? Grace didn't want to imagine. It might be a season of bitter cold.

Grace possessed both faith and hope. She knew that God loved them. She had seen how God had taken care of them since they'd been home. *"God is good,"* Grace quieted herself.

Faith, hope and love. The Bible tells us that these are the three greatest things. All other things will pass away, but these three will remain. These three things Grace certainly had.

....

Though he grew strong, David never developed the coordination of other children his age. It wasn't readily noticeable. However, when it came time to swim or to skip or jump rope or ride a bike, nothing came easy.

Most children were learning how to do these things while David was still falling off of his chair, head first. When Honorah, was four, she taught herself to swim. When David was four, he was undergoing chemotherapy. When Moriah and Nicholas were six, they learned to ride a bike. David used training wheels till he was almost nine because he couldn't keep his balance.

He never did learn how to skip.

"I understand that he might be behind in language skills, and, maybe a little behind in motor skills, but why does he struggle so much with these simple things?" Grace agonized over David's progress. *"He is socially on target. He can do math. He can read. He's bright. But he can't tie his shoes. He can't write neatly. He can't skip. It's taking him forever to learn to ride a bike."*

By the age of eight David had grown into his once oversized head. It no longer looked too big for his body. His arms were able to reach around it. Top heavy no longer, David could sit up from a lying position. The size and weight of his head no longer factored into his ability to run and play. Still he struggled with simple tasks.

The root of his struggles became clear to Grace one bright summer day shortly after David's eighth birthday. The children were swimming in the pool and David was copying them, teaching himself to swim. He did well. Grace was proud of him. Round and round he swam in a circle. As Grace watched, it dawned on her that David was only using one arm.

"One arm!" Grace stood up on the deck. One arm! He's only using one arm. It's because of the strokes. He's stronger on one side than the other.

"Use both hands, honey." Grace leaned over the rail. *"You'll go straight."*

David listened and used both arms. He did go straight, straighter than he had before. This was a milestone for David as well as the rest of the family. Now that they knew the cause of his motor delays, they were better equipped to help David with everyday tasks. Swimming in the pool that summer strengthened David more equally on both sides. After learning to swim, David mastered his bicycle. He learned to tie his shoes. Small things became easier. Each small triumph was a witness to the healing power of prayer.

By age nine David had conquered skiing. It took more lessons than the average nine year old takes, but

David's legs were becoming strong. They were strong enough to make a wedge with his skis and turn at will. David had changed from a frail, sickly, wisp of a child into a strong, normal, healthy boy in almost every sense of the word.

David's bouts with asthma grew less and less as the years progressed. The Hep B alone remained a problem. This was the work of prayer. The power of God brings change through prayer.

But it isn't always easy.

Mark and Grace got David's blood work done in the middle of February, 2009. It took till the middle of March to get in to the specialist. David had seemed much healthier lately. He had gone longer and longer between bouts of asthma. By the time he was ten years old he hadn't needed the nebulizer in years. He seemed healthy in body and sound of mind. Grace and Mark eagerly awaited the results of his blood work.

This time David's viral load was 1,783,000. Almost two million parts of virus per milliliter of blood; it was a very big number. It was still way too high for antibodies to begin to form let alone take over. Still, it was the lowest number David had ever had.

Grace had been prepared for a miracle. She had her heart set on a miracle. She was severely disappointed. *"Where is the miracle, God?"* Grace lowered her head and muttered at the Lord.

"You didn't pray for a miracle, you prayed for healing."

"I prayed for a healing miracle."

"And you got it."

Grace looked at the numbers again. David's numbers had been over 2 billion six months earlier. At 1.78 million they were less than one percent of what they had been six months ago; Less than 1 percent. That meant that over 99 percent of the virus was gone. One million, seven hundred eighty three thousand is a big number, but not compared to two billion. With 99 percent of the virus gone, what was another one percent? Nothing is impossible with God.

"Ok God," Grace conceded gratefully, *"I see your healing hand in this. Thanks. And please help me to find just a little more patience."*

Suddenly a cold thought struck her. It chilled her to the bone. Where had all that virus gone? David's liver was already hardening. If his liver had strained out this much virus it might have hardened beyond repair. That was the liver's job – to strain out the virus. And that's what causes the liver to harden – being clogged with virus.

"His liver?" Grace pressed the doctor. Panic was rising in her throat. *"What about his liver?"*

"His body has begun to fight the disease," the doctor explained. *"The liver numbers are not too abnormal. The body is doing the work. In fact his allergy numbers are down. He used to have tremendously high allergy numbers, but they are way down now."*

"The asthma," Grace thought. *"No wonder we haven't needed the inhaler. His body is healing itself. No, not healing itself, God is healing him. A healing miracle! David is being healed all over. Not just his Hep B, but also the asthma; the effects of the syphilis and the rickets and the strokes as well. It is a healing miracle. God is so good. He always does more than you could think or ask for. Always so much more than you expect. Always a better 'yes'."*

The doctor lifted David onto the table and pressed on David's liver with her well practiced fingers. *"Still soft and pliable,"* she assured Mark and Grace. *"No liver biopsy necessary this time."*

"Good." They both sighed in unison. "Good."

"Just patience," she said. *"We'll wait to see what happens. If his liver does start to harden then we can do clinical trials with new medications that are coming on the market. If his numbers keep coming down there are antiviral medications that can help move things along. But the antiviral medications destroy the kidneys, so letting the body heal itself is best. It's up to you to decide which method of treatment you wish to pursue."*

"Patience," Mark and Grace echoed in agreement. "We will absolutely wait to see what happens." After that terrible year on Chemo they were no longer eager to use aggressive treatment of any sort. It was patience that the Lord had been calling them to and patience that they would now practice.

They had the faith to wait for David's healing. They knew God was moving in this. They knew He loved

David and had a plan for him. Like his mother before them, hope was renewed.

Faith, hope and love. These three things had been planted in their lives as tiny seeds. Each seed grew with every new encounter with the Lord. It was as God had intended.

If God had healed David as an infant, then Mark and Grace would never have been able to adopt him. If God had healed David as soon as they brought him home, they would have praised God and perhaps forgotten about it. Just another miracle; but God had a different plan. His plan was this book. His plan was to show everyone that He has a future and a hope for those who will turn to the Lord.

If you are reading this book then you are part of His plan. His plan is that you would know first about salvation. The minute you ask Jesus into your life you are a new creation. You may or may not feel like a new creation, but you are. Accept Him. He has accepted you.

The second thing that God would have you know is the power of prayer. Prayer is talking to God – just like you would talk to a friend. He is your friend. He wants to talk with you. He wants to show you new things. Ask Him into your life - then talk to Him.

Another thing God wants you to know is how much He loves you. He created you. Nothing you have done can make God hate you. Just ask for forgiveness. God is love. Love forgives all things. And forgive yourself. See yourself as God does.

God wants you to read your Bible and see all the blessings He has given to other people. These are the same blessings He has for you. All the blessings that Mark and Grace and their family walk in – these blessings are for you also. God loves to bless His children. Find your blessings. Claim them.

God also wants you to read your Bible so that you can find out what God expects of you. You should earnestly desire to know the way of God and the will of God for your life. Seek after Him.

If you realize how much God loves you and take a step of faith and ask Jesus to be part of your life, then you have just planted the seeds of faith and love. You have hope for the future. These three things, faith, hope and love will grow in you with each encounter you have with God. Grow in these things. Raise your children in these things.

The Bible tells us not to forsake the gathering together of believers. Gather together. Be a witness to one another of what God has done in your life. Be encouragers. Love the Lord and each other. Serve God by helping others.

We all have a choice. We can be part of God's plan – or not. If you want what He is offering you – forgiveness for sins, eternal life in heaven, love, blessings, relationship with the one true God, an ever present help in time of need, a future and a hope, for yourself and for your children, then tell Him right now. He's waiting to hear from you.

"'For I know the plans I have for you,' says the Lord. 'They are for good and not for evil, to give you a

future and a hope. In those days, when you pray I will listen. If you look for me in earnest, you will find me when you seek me. I will be found by you,' says the Lord. 'I will end your captivity and restore your fortunes.'" Jeremiah 29:11-14a

CHAPTER XIX

Faith – The Substance of Things Hoped For

As of September 2009 David's viral load had dropped to 341,000 ppml. It was 80% less than his last test six months before. It was now at a level where antibodies could begin to develop.

His next blood test was taken in August of 2010. In September Grace and Mark met with the doctors. The results were what they'd been waiting for all these years. David's body had finally developed antibodies. His body was fighting the Hepatitis B.

"This is good? Right?" Grace bubbled over. She was ecstatic. *"Antibodies! That's what we've been waiting for! This is it! We're done! Right?"*

"No," the doctor replied. *"David still has a viral load of 85,000 ppm. That's less than point five percent (0.05%) than the two billion ppm that he started with, but still, the viral load needs to be zero before we can say he is cured. The antibodies may not be doing their job. If that's the case he will be harder to cure."*

"But he could be in transition. He may just still be in the middle of fighting the rest of the virus," Grace

said. "All we need to do is wait a few months and check again. He could be cured."

"Yes. That could be the case." The doctor weighed his words. "However, his liver enzyme numbers are very high. We can't allow them to remain that high for too long. If we wait too long, he can develop cancer. We can only wait a few more months before we have to begin treating him again."

"Cancer?" Grace froze for a moment. She'd expected the best. She always expected the best. "How's his liver? Is it hardening?"

The doctor palpated his liver. "It's still soft and pliable."

Grace breathed a sigh of relief. David's liver was fine. His viral load was still coming down. His enzymes were up, but he was still fighting this disease. It was OK. They could wait. Grace had learned that waiting for the good things of the Lord was OK. She could do it. She had faith, not hope, but faith. She had pure, absolute faith in God. God is the God who heals us. He had been healing David for years. He didn't suddenly stop. He was still healing David. She could wait a few more months.

"There are some new medicines I want you to research and get comfortable with in case we have to begin treatment," the doctor continued.

Mark wrote down the names of the medications they were to research. He gathered the paperwork for the new blood work to be done in a few months. Grace just nodded at the doctor. She wasn't listening. There was no need for her to look into treatments. God was still healing David. He just hadn't finished yet. Grace had heard the only word she had needed to hear - 'antibodies'.

"*Have a nice day!*" Mark and Grace called to the doctor as they left her office.

"*See you in a few months,*" was her cheery reply.

"*Antibodies! He has antibodies!*" Grace thought to herself. "*God has given him antibodies. That test was taken in August. This is the end of September. He could be healed right now.*" No other possibilities were permitted to cloud her day.

"*Whose report will you believe?*" God gently whispered encouragement in her ear. She knew in her heart that David was healed. Faith is the substance of things hoped for.

The doctor may have needed another three months to find this out. He may need another three years. Grace didn't. She began to praise God immediately.

"*Thank you Lord for the antibodies; please touch them and jumpstart them if they are not doing their job. All it takes is your touch. And please bring the liver enzyme numbers down to normal. You are such an awesome God. Thank you so much. Thank you for healing David. Thank you for loving David. Thank you for having a plan for David. Thank you for loving us all. Lord, what would we do without you?*"

In her mind Grace pictured a giant hand running through David's body. It was the healing hand of God. She had seen it before when she'd prayed for a friend – and that friend had been healed. Grace knew that she knew that she knew that God was healing David. She floated home on a cloud of pure joy produced by unwavering faith. David was healed.

"We need to give him back to the Lord," she told Mark. *"We need to fill him full of the scripture and give him back to the Lord. He is a walking testimony of what the Lord has done."*

Mark readily agreed. *"We can do that,"* he said. *"It'll be our next adventure."*

CHAPTER XX

Update

In August of 2011 David's viral load was 4200 ppml.

By January of 2012 David's viral load was 1200 ppml.

By June of 2016 David's viral load was untraceable. Complete remission.

David's liver enzyme numbers are very near normal. The antibodies are slowly doing their job.

Grace is still waiting patiently for David's complete recovery. Her patience is no longer filled with fear and doubt and worry. Her patience is filled with joy and with deep gratitude. She knows that the Lord loves her. She knows that the Lord loves David. She knows that God is a healer. She knows that prayer changes things. And she knows that God has a plan – for every one of us.

Interestingly enough, David's healings came in many shapes and sizes. Hydrocephalous and Hep C were either instantly cured or misdiagnosed. Grace is of the opinion that the hydrocephalous was misdiagnosed and Hep C was miraculously cured as he had tested positive for it several times.

Syphilis was cured medicinally.

Ricketts was cured with sunshine and vitamin D.

Seizures and strokes never occurred again.

Curvature of the spine was outgrown over time. This is a healing miracle which took time.

Asthma has been outgrown over time.

The Hep B viral load is still unaccountably low.

Grace praises God for every healing, no matter how it comes.

Grace's own healing came over time. She and David are now both healthy and strong and pressing into the Lord for new adventures.

ABOUT THE AUTHOR

Nancy Brown is the mother of six boys and three girls, and a multitude of spiritual children. She is now also Grammy to six beautiful girls and three handsome little boys. Her children and grandchildren are scattered all over the US and Korea, but David still lives at home with her and Mark in Moravian Falls, NC.

Mark and Nancy raised their family in Stroudsburg, PA, where they owned and operated a building supply business for over 20 years. They stepped into missions through YWAM after the business was sold. Nancy's heart for Mongolia led them there to serve as missionaries for several years immediately following their YWAM adventure. Mark and Nancy later studied under Randy Clark at Global Awakening in Mechanicsburg, PA, before moving to Moravian Falls, NC.

Here in Moravian Falls, they run Apple Hill Lodge (www.AppleHillLodgeNC.com) through More Ministries (www.MoreMoravianFalls.com) with their partners Frank and Susan Starr. They continue to seek after more of the Lord. They continue to pray for healings and miracles. They continue to see the hand of the Lord at work in mighty ways.

It is Mark and Nancy's goal to reach and teach people of all ages about the awesome 'MORE' of God.

GLOSSARY

Aichy – Mom

Aimag – county

Buuz – national dish made of beef and pastry

Gher – traditional Mongolian home – a circular tent made of wool

Holshuur – traditional dish made of beef and pastry

Morin Khur – horsehead fiddle – made with two strings

Owa – Dad

Ulaan Baator – Mongolia's capitol city

Made in the USA
Monee, IL
05 April 2022